ETERNAL
DHARMA

ETERNAL DHARMA

How to Find Spiritual Evolution
Through Surrender and
Embrace Your Life's True Purpose

VISHNU SWAMI

The Maverick Monk

New Page Books
A Division of The Career Press, Inc
Wayne, NJ

ETERNAL DHARMA
EDITED BY JODI BRANDON
TYPESET BY PERFECTYPE, NASHVILLE, TENNESSEE
Cover design by Ian Shimkoviak/ thebook designers
Cover image by WICHAI WONGJONGJAIHAN/shutterstock
Printed in the U.S.A.

To order this title, please call toll-free 1-800-CAREER-1 (NJ and Canada: 201-848-0310) to order using VISA or MasterCard, or for further information on books from Career Press.

The Career Press, Inc.
12 Parish Drive
Wayne, NJ 07470
www.careerpress.com

Library of Congress Cataloging-in-Publication Data

CIP Data Available Upon Request.

DEDICATION

I dedicate this book to the most important person in my life: my beloved
Guru, Srila Bhaktivedanta Narayan Goswami Maharaja.
It is only by His loving guidance and affectionate mentorship
that I feel that I am able to understand, advance, and grow on this
ever-sweet spiritual path.

ACKNOWLEDGMENTS

First, I express my gratitude and affection to my most beloved Guru Srila Bhaktivedanta Narayana Maharaja. He is my life and soul; I am forever grateful to Him and Srila Bhaktivedanta Swami Prabhupada for all that they have created and taught. It is only because of them that I am on this spiritual path and I love them dearly.

As I write this, I am humbled and elated at the sheer thought of the divine masters of my beautiful Gaudiya lineage. My gurus come from a rich lineage of spiritual preceptors, all of which have given invaluable and unique insights to the spiritual path and spiritual domain. I offer my respects and gratitude to all of them.

I thank all the members of Iskcon and the Gaudiya Math and all Vaishnavas of the past, present, and future. Though as a maverick I have my qualms with certain cultural approaches to the spiritual, it is a fact that I would know nothing of the spiritual without having had the sweet association of the various Vaishnava communities. I am forever grateful to them.

I would like express my deepest appreciation to Bill Gladstone, my wise and inspired book agent, whose guidance and support in this endeavor of creating *Eternal Dharma* has been invaluable. He continues to surprise me with his wisdom. Rick Freshman is a ball of energy and book production genius. Thank you for helping catapult this book to the next level.

Thank you Michael, Adam, Lauren, and all the wonderful people at New Page Books. You have been fabulous and tolerant. I admire your clarity and tenacity in bringing this book to market in the best possible light. Michael, your mentorship was amazing; and Lauren, thank you! A little blurb like this is too short to express my admiration and appreciation for everyone at New Page who so diligently have done everything to make this book wonderful, so I will just send you all one big thank you!

Thank you to Berny Dohrmann and my CEO Space family.

To my friend Joel Roberts, what can I say? Thank you just does not do it. You dug deep into me and inspired and guided me on how to share my core with the world at large. You are a communication master. Thank you!

I could write a book on how cool everyone who was key in creating *Eternal Dharma* is. But we will keep it short, for you have a mind-blowing book to read.

Sita, Rasik Mohan, Devananda, Mallika, Acyutananda, Nityananda, Daniela, Dr. Woody, Dr. Jonathan Glass, and BV Vaikhanas Maharaja, thank you for your thoughts and insights to my writing.

Sripad Premananda Prabhu, BV Madhava Maharaja, BV Tirtha Maharaja, BV Sridhar Maharaja, Srimati Syamarani Didi, Harold (Hari), Lani, Alexandr Aguet, Racitambara Mataji, Veda Sara, Alex Carrol, all our Gaudiya Sanyasis, and all other monks and friends and supporters, thank you for being an inspiration, guide, and friend.

CONTENTS

Introduction: Welcome: A Spiritual Journey 11

PART 1: FOUNDATIONAL KNOWLEDGE

Chapter 1: Inherent Function: The Principle of Dharma 25

Chapter 2: Finding Your Dharma 41

Chapter 3: Spiritual Surrender and Integration 53

PART 2: THE UNPRECEDENTED ELEMENTAL REALITY SYSTEM

Chapter 4: Introducing the Unprecedented Elemental Reality System . 71

Chapter 5: Elemental Foundations 83

Chapter 6: Earth's Steadiness, Water's Flavor, and Fire's Passion 97

Chapter 7: The Power of Air—Prana—Chi. 115

Chapter 8: The Serenity of Ether 127

Chapter 9: The Echoing Mind. 137

Chapter 10: The Calculations of Intelligence. 151

Chapter 11: The Hidden Power of Identity 165

Chapter 12: Creating and Using the Elements as a System. 179

PART 3: THE DHARMA OF THE DIVINE

Chapter 13: The Constitutional Nature of the Soul:
  Dharma of the Soul 201

Chapter 14: The 3 Stages of Spiritual Evolution. 215

Chapter 15: The 3 Stages of Enlightenment and the Divine 225

Chapter 16: A Loving Relationship With the Divine 237

Chapter 17: How to Grow Spiritual Love. 249

Next Steps 261

Index. 263

WELCOME:
A SPIRITUAL JOURNEY

My dear friend, welcome. You are about to embark on a splendid journey. I applaud you, for not everyone is willing or ready to embark on such a spiritual journey. By simply opening a book entitled *Eternal Dharma*, you have already earned my respect, for it takes a special kind of person to be looking to grow both spiritually and practically.

You probably have already begun your spiritual journey. You probably have begun to introspect and search to find meaning, connection, clarity, purpose, and inspiration in life. Yet, I am 99.99 percent confident that wherever you are on your spiritual path you will find this book helpful, because the wisdom, tools, and practices presented here are both ancient and unique.

I anticipate that in our time together a lot will happen. We are going to cover a lot of ground, some of which will be light and imbued with warm and fun feelings of felicity. Some will be deeply philosophical, dealing with the fundamental questions of life that have plagued thinkers, philosophers, and spiritual seekers for millennia. All of what we cover will be practical, and is designed to immediately empower you in both Effective Action and on your path to passionate enlightenment.

Perfecting Effective Action

We often feel powerless. We have many desires we wish to fulfill. We want tangible results, such as more cash, better health, more time, and sweeter relationships; and many of us are constantly seeking new, better, and more effective ways to execute our plans. Many of us are seeking how we can better live, be, and do things in the world. We seek new tool sets, tricks, and mindsets so that we can be much more effective.

A question we may ask is: What can I learn that will increase my effectiveness to create better results in my life and business, while having a more joyful experience in the process? I believe that the 5,000-year-old spiritual wisdom of India presented here in this book is the ultimate, best, and most powerful system for Effective Action. Being a continual student of self-help, personal growth, and business effectiveness has been very helpful, but never left me completely satisfied. I wanted a system of understanding life and effectiveness that was complete—that took everything in existence into account.

"Everything in existence" is quite vast. There are physical things that you can touch and measure, such as earth, water, airplanes, rocks, houses, and so forth. There are also subtle things such as emotions, ideas, information, and desires. "All of existence" also includes galaxies, business, relationships, economies, brands, healthcare, actions, plans, music, events, the spiritual domain, rubber duckies, and chocolate bars. In reality all of these things exist together in the same world, in unison, and in reasonable harmony. I wanted a knowledge system that acknowledged and capitalized on this natural coexistence.

The Lost Key in Personal Empowerment

There many systems in the world: There are health systems like yoga, acupuncture, and neurosurgery. There are fighting systems like jujitsu and swordsmanship. There are knowledge systems such as architecture, race car driving, scuba diving, war, politics, sex, business, investing, agriculture, astrology, astronomy, and education. I wanted a personal growth and empowerment system to work in synergistic unison—in harmony with all these other knowledge systems. I wanted to find the intrinsic truths that prevail in all things in existence and all knowledge systems of the world.

On top of that, I wanted a personal empowerment knowledge system that made philosophical sense and also harmonized with the often-elusive spiritual domain. I also wanted a system that was not just based on any one person's experience or a little bit of research, but one that had more depth, preferably thousands of years of verification and the input of many enlightened masters. This way I could ultimately trust the system and use it with confidence.

When I looked back on the ancient spiritual training I received as a child in the monastery, I found such a complete, powerful, and unique system that not only worked superbly, but made so much sense. After becoming aware of this system as a tool for both self-help and spiritual growth, I spent another eight years researching practicing and refining this knowledge to present it to you today.

My Journey of Dharma and Surrender

As my body was burning I could not stop crying. It was the most agony I had ever felt. More emotional turmoil than I knew was possible pumped through my arteries. As my stomach churned in anguish I was unable to eat or sleep. This was that dreaded low point in life. My project and financial support were stolen from me. My Guru, who is my life and soul, the most important person to me, had just departed from this world. The only girl I had ever had a relationship with and that I loved fully, had moved on. Due to my conscious choice to defy social expectations, rumors were rampant, and I felt shunned, rejected, and unloved by the spiritual community I had lived in for my entire life. I had nothing. Everything I had created was lost. I lay there alone, wailing and screaming in pain, with my heart grated into shreds, melting in a box, hungry, with no fan in the center of summer in the hottest inhabitable place on planet Earth.

At this low point, I had to decide: What was I going to do? Who was I going to be to get out of that pitiful mess? I had studied the law of attraction, but it seemed to only attract pain. I tried to be present in the moment, but all the moments of that time were torturous. Affirmations felt like fibbing, and business books did not help. I had studied all the self-help work, but still, it simply did not work.

In truth, this period of persistent pain was one of the greatest blessings of my life. It put me in a situation where I had to clearly choose: Did I want to live my Eternal Dharma, did I want to take the risk to surrendering spiritually and apply all the 5,000-year-old spiritual wisdom that I had been trained in for my entire life, or did I want to give it all up and move forward without giving credence to the spiritual domain? I chose dharma. I chose to surrender—to surrender fully, with no hope or expectation, just to surrender in love—and magic began to unfold! You see, there are different qualities of spiritual action, and though I had been trying to serve and surrender spiritually for the majority of my life, this time, due to the intensity of the situation and where I was in my spiritual evolution, I surrendered in a way that I had not done before. I gave up all other hope, backup, or plans. I gave up any expectation of societal approval, acceptance, or even any expectation of my basic human needs of food, shelter, and connection. I simply offered myself to the divine through the peaceful intensity of dharmic action, and this is when the magic of Spiritual Surrender really began to flow.

This time around, the choice to surrender was especially significant. It was a choice to live my full dharma, and in a sense it knocked me out of my previous fairytale-like life.

You see, at the age of 11, I moved into a monastery in India. It was off in a distant Eastern land. We lived in mud huts with thatched roofs, and the grounds had lush gardens that bloomed with tropical flowers. These gardens were embellished with large quartz crystals, colored stone that pulsated with a flare of Eastern design. Mango, banana, and palm trees covered the land, and everything seemed complete. We even had a pet elephant (who stripped me once, but that's a comical story for another time). Thousands gathered to view our weekly ceremonial processions, which included dance with music, elephants, fireworks, and mystic rituals. We woke daily at 2:45 a.m. to start meditating, perform ancient spiritual rituals, and vibrate spiritual sound in song. Daily we trained in memorizing and rigorously studying the ancient Vedic texts, which embody the 5,000-year-old spiritual wisdom of India. This was the context of my childhood and teenage years.

Later, after this experience, I traveled under the direct guidance and mentorship of my Guru, Srila Bhaktivedanta Narayan Goswami Maharaja—one of the greatest bhakti-yoga masters of our time. He bestowed upon me the greatest honor by making me the youngest swami, at only age 23.

A swami is the most revered monk authority position in the spiritual traditions of India. He sent me on five continents, in 20 countries to teach and 80 cities around the world. I taught internationally in universities, five-star hotels, million-dollar condos, and simple village mud huts in the most likely place in the world to be eaten by a tiger. Crowds as large as 15,000 would sometimes gather to hear me speak.

Life Is Not Cheap: I Need More Proof

But this would not do. Simply having pretty gardens, an elephant, 5,000 years of wisdom, and a large international audience was not enough to convince me of the validity of this knowledge system. To this day I am shocked how people can so quickly and easily accept a way of thinking without challenging and verification. For the 20 years of my monastic training I did two things: I simultaneously followed, practiced, and served with all my heart, soul, body, and mind, while at the same time I challenged and tried to find any weakness or falsity in each teaching. Life is not cheap, I only get to live this one once, and it shall not be governed by arbitrary ideas, rules, or expectation of a bound society; I want only heart-quenching eternal truth. Therefore, my continual ideological challenging, combined with sincere spiritual exploration and practice, let me shed much of tradition, mental fabrication, and the customs that are often taught as spiritual truth. At the same time I got to cultivate a powerful spiritual connection with the divine.

But still, even though internally I was detached from tradition and culture, I was bound to it. I had a societal role to play and I was comfortable. My ego was big and because of this I was losing my connection with the Divine.

This low point in my life, during which I felt immeasurable pain, is what gave me the wake-up call to only accept what I found to be spiritualessence, while at the same time giving less credence to the customs and traditions and societal pressures that often accompany any spiritual or religious teaching. This is one of the reasons why I am now known as the Maverick Monk. I simply teach what I have found to be essential spiritual truth and thus I don't represent any church, religion, cult, or institution.

For You

I want what is best for you, and therefore I am writing this book. I found that the crux of all the 5,000-year-old spiritual wisdom of the East is to know your Eternal Dharma, and I sincerely want you to be able to access it and taste the sweetness of bliss and practical effectiveness it can provide. I intend for this book to save you 20 years of monastic living and a whole bunch of heartbreak and pain.

Why learn spiritual wisdom? What will we get out of it? Here are a few reasons.

Life can be tough. Sometimes we lose our jobs, our businesses are underfunded, or we may become sick. We sometimes feel heartbreak and go through gut-jolting breakups. We get into fights and get stuck in traffic jams, our loved ones die, and friends can betray us. Like one of my Gurus used to say, "This world is not a fit place for a gentleman." True spiritual wisdom is that wisdom which guides and supports us through these troubling times. True spiritual wisdom is not put to the test when everything is going well. True spiritual wisdom is seen in those hardest times of life, those times that can cripple us, those times that drive us to tears, those time that bring us to our knees and cause us to throw our arms up in the air and scream, "Why me? Why am I suffering in this way?" Spiritual wisdom gives us solace that supports and uplifts us, even when we feel angry, sad, disappointed, or hurt. In reality, true spiritual wisdom is the bedrock of truth that eases our pain, guides us to Effective Action, and propels us to joy when life gets tough.

On my world-teaching tours I have come into contact with hundreds of thousands of people. I have found that there are three basic heart pains that are running rampant throughout humanity. These pains are extremely deep, yet most people learn to ignore or deny their existence because they do not know what to do about them.

1. **Deep down inside they are afraid of being alone and don't have the deep connection they crave.**

We all crave love and connection, but, in truth, we know that whatever love we taste cannot stay the same: the connection will end (by death at best) and therefore it cannot truly satisfy us. There is a certain everlasting union that our soul desperately cries for. Our relationships may come close to this union, but they never fulfill that need completely. We feel alone and empty in the inner core of our being and continuously try to fill that void with relationships, family, friends, socializing, success, media, and sensory pleasures. We try to cover the pain of what seems like the truth of our existence: We are alone.

2. **Life is not fully satisfying. Inside they know that there should be more, or that something is missing.**

We have so many desires, and many of them go unfulfilled. The strange thing is that even the desires that do get fulfilled don't really satisfy us. In our heart we believe that we are meant to taste more. We are meant to be satisfied and fulfilled—made happy by life—but the truth is, despite all our accomplishments and fortune, we still suffer tremendously. Our wants still go unmet, and for every ounce of pleasure, there is a pound of pain. True happiness seems just around the corner, almost attainable, but the fact is: Our existence is more dominated by suffering than anything else.

3. **Deep down inside they don't know what life is about and therefore don't know what to do with it.**

Life can be a complex mess. The truth is that most people still don't deeply understand what this life thing is all about and how to really be happy in it. Therefore, they get stuck in a mediocre existence, unable to truly excel to perfection. In their hearts they wish and know that life, this world, and all of existence, should make sense. There must be a better way! But they simply do not know the nature of life. They may fool themselves into pretending that they got it, yet their inner heart pains them, and they feel lost.

Spiritual Wisdom Tickles Our Spirits

But wait! Spiritual wisdom is not only for those who are suffering; it is not merely meant to help us navigate through troubling times. True spiritual wisdom is the guiding light that not only tickles our spirits, but inundates our soul with sweetness. Imagine if, in every action you took, you felt a loving care warmer than the love of a thousand mothers. Imagine every so-called boring, mundane, monotonous action, like driving to work, filling your heart with more loving joy than when you first held your baby in your arms. Imagine a simple action such as crossing the road becoming more pleasurable than your best orgasm. Imagine brushing your teeth in such a way that you connect with the source of all spiritual bliss. This would make teeth-brushing more thrilling than bungee-jumping from Mount Everest. When connected in deep spiritual wisdom, you will be able to see more beauty in a simple pebble than most will ever see in their lover's face. When situated in pure Spiritual Surrender, the resplendent joy of simply uttering a word in spiritual mantra will inundate your being with the most effervescent bliss ever relished.

Our Higher Purpose

Yes, by bettering yourself with this 5,000-year-old spiritual wisdom, you will be able to eradicate your pain and suffering. Yes, you will be empowered to magnify your effectiveness in all areas of your life. And yes, you will be able to inundate your being with the most effervescent bliss ever relished. But one of the best reasons to embark on such a spiritual journey is simply because this is you. The core essence of your being is divinely spiritual. Therefore, any way of being that is not operating from this core is missing the point. Most of us have lost touch with our spiritual essence and therefore have lost touch with ourselves. We walk through life without knowing the true core of our being. Our lives may be filled with certain joys and woes, but our current conditioned, covered-over quality of being, will never be fully bright, beautiful, and powerful, unless we bring forth and shine our spiritual essence. Living from our core spiritual essence is our duty and reason for being alive. Though we may have some awareness of this, that awareness is incomplete until we genuinely identify significantly more with our spiritual self than with our conditioned body and mind. This may sound simple, but it is no cheap feat; it is a process that takes at least a lifetime.

More Tangible Than Sex

If our higher essence, our soul, is spiritual, then our experience of the spiritual dimension will be much more tangible than our identification with our body and mind. Spirituality is not imagination or fantasy. I say that if relationships in this world can be as measurably tangible as physical sex, then a relationship with the Divine or "God," as some would say, should be at least as measurably tangible as sex. In actuality, the experience should be even more real.

When we truly understand that it is our birthright, our duty, and our constitutional nature to always taste the supremely sweet joy of divine love, we cannot help but use every inch of our being to constantly swim in the seductive sweetness of pure spiritual unity. Such happiness is spiritual life; it is the essence of all wisdom. If any endeavor does not lead to such continual tasting of bliss, it is cheating us. Why settle for less than swimming in the unadulterated rapture of supreme spiritual serenity? After all, this is who you are, it is your birthright, and the sole cause for your existence on this planet.

No Himalayan Cave Necessary

There is a prevalent idea that the ideal spiritual person is the one who leaves the world behind, a detached monastic who lives in a cave in the Himalayas, who does not work and has no money, family, friends, or business. This idea says that the world is somehow impure and bad, and that being worldly is the complete opposite of being spiritual. I disagree with this, and the 5,000-year-old spiritual wisdom of Veda shows little support of this idea. As you know, I did live in a monastery in the jungles of West Bengal beginning when I was 11 years old. I found that it is not the world which is bad or impure, nor that acting in the world is bad. Our relationship with the world and our relationship with action is what counts. Any action can either help us grow and advance on our spiritual journey, or can derail us from our spiritual path. Just like eating: In and of itself, eating is neither good nor bad; it's just eating. It needs no glorification or condemnation. You have the choice to eat in a way that nourishes and supports you, or in a way that destroys you. Living and acting in the world is the same way: It can either bind you and cause tremendous suffering, or it can liberate you. On the spiritual path, more often than not, we don't need to change most of our actions, we just need to change our relationship with them and thus infuse them with transcendental love.

The Enlightened Yogi

Yoga has become popular in the world, and now millions of people are reaping the many health and stress-relieving benefits of yoga. People know that yoga goes hand-in-hand with meditation, and many people also know that yoga is somehow intertwined with the spiritual. The unfortunate truth is that despite the immense popularity of yoga, the knowledge of how yoga is actually interrelated with the spiritual domain is practically non-existent in the Western world. Most of the spiritual aspects of yoga are left to speculation and superficiality.

Yoga is a complete holistic science meant to better the whole individual. The health and fitness aspect is only a small, or perhaps the smallest, aspect of the yoga system. According to the 5,000-year-old Vedic wisdom of India of which yoga is a part, the true purpose of yoga is to lead to enlightenment, which is a far greater attainment than the mere peacefulness, vibrant health, and a sexy, toned body that yoga is known to provide. This book will guide you through high-level yoga concepts and meditation practices that will speedily lead you to enlightenment. Yoga has the spiritual intertwined into the core of its practice, but commercialization and lack of proper education have derailed mainstream yoga from its original and most potent form. If you want to get the most out of yoga and reap the best benefits yoga can offer, you must walk the spiritual the path of Enlightenment.

I want you to be able to savor and experience the sweet serenity of Spiritual Surrender. My friend, I want you to know your deepest Eternal Dharma and have the ability to practically use this unique and ancient wisdom for better results in your life and business. So this book is not just theory, it is filled with practices, meditations, and practical guides.

Yes, there are many new intellectual ideas presented in this book that will excite any thoughtful mind, but this book is also designed to guide you in your spiritual pilgrimage to passionate enlightenment. It is not to solely arouse your mind with fresh intellectual rational. As the saying goes, "An ounce of practice is worth a ton of theory."

I know that both in the spiritual and personal growth worlds, often the same information is regurgitated into new books and programs. This book is not that. The information presented here, though grounded in 5,000 years of wisdom, is new and fresh.

A Delicious Three-Course Meal

This book can be thought of as a three-course meal. Part 1 is the appetizer and is filled with foundational concepts to prepare you for Part 2. Part 2 is the main course and the bulk of the book. Part 3 is dessert, which is about the sweetness of the Divine. In this meal we have a sweet tooth, and savoring dessert is the real motivation for sitting at this illustrious meal table.

In each chapter, I give you some simple actions to take. This will help you integrate what you have learned. In this way, what you have learned will become a part of your core being. The exercises provided here will serve as a tool to help turn the information of this book into realized knowledge. Thus this 5,000-year-old wisdom will always be there for you, nourishing, supporting, and empowering you when you need it. This path and practice of dharma is the way of the ancients, and though thousands before you have walked this deep path, your journey will be unique, because you are unique.

The actions I have selected for you in this book may be as simple as taking a few minutes to contemplate an idea and see how it works in your life. It may be an exercise or meditation to bring you into deeper touch with your core self. I may also provide some practical tips to make you more effective in executing projects and business ventures. I may also suggest some adjustments to your habits to help you create a better life.

Mantras, which are a special set of words often used in mediation, are known to hold great power and are like keys that can assist in unlocking the many mysteries of life. Throughout this training program, I will reveal some of the ancient secret mantras that have been enclosed in hidden monasteries and only taught to select spiritual practitioners. They have been passed down in special lineages and will give you a special boost.

I have every intention for this book to be the best guidebook possible to shorten your path to enlightenment and to empower you to perform the most Effective Action humanly possible. My dear friend, your journey is about to begin. I am honored to be there with you and to support and guide you along the way. Only power, love, joy, and deep understanding await you. Go forth and conquer! Soon, you shall be one of the fortunate few to swim in the soothing waves of the sweet serenity of Spiritual Surrender. I could not be happier for you!

PART 1

FOUNDATIONAL KNOWLEDGE

CHAPTER 1

INHERENT FUNCTION: THE PRINCIPLE OF DHARMA

Welcome. I am Vishnu Swami, the one they call the Maverick Monk, and though we have not met in person, I look forward to assisting and guiding you on your spiritual journey throughout this book.

Life can sometimes be a tough and complicated mess; navigating through it is a challenge we all face. Luckily the great kings, thinkers, and enlightened beings of the past have left us with a treasure trove of wisdom that not only can help us make sense of life, but practically empowers us to live effectively, powerfully, and in passionate, blissful spiritual serenity.

This book has two goals. The first is to guide you in your spiritual evolution so that you can progress to the highest states of pure Passionate Enlightenment. The second is to guide you in Effective Action so that you can achieve all that you want in life, be it a flourishing business, a passionate relationship, or a vibrant physique.

You see, my friend, what differentiates me from most monks is that I don't believe that you have to negate the material to attain the spiritual.

Through a lifetime of practice, study, and the best spiritual mentorship, I have found that both the spiritual and material domains are integrated and mutually supportive, and growth in one of these domains can profoundly help support the other.

As discussed in the Introduction, Part 1 of this book is like an appetizer, in which we will learn key foundational concepts that are fundamentally important for achieving our two goals of Effective Action and Passionate Enlightenment. Part 2 of this book is akin to the main course, in which we get more practical, and learn the Unprecedented Elemental Reality System. We will roll up our sleeves and tweak our life to perfection. Part 3 is like the dessert, in which we fully hone into the spiritual domain and explore it with a level of depth and perspective that is sure to boost any spiritual seeker into a new dimension of passionately inspired love and sweetness.

My friend, let's get started.

The Wisdom of the Ancients: Veda

For many thousands of years, sages and scholars have been contemplating the complexities and purpose of life. About 5,000 years ago, a body of texts was compiled, illuminating every facet of life. This body of wisdom is known as Veda. It was closely guarded and taught from Guru to disciple, and its secrets were kept hidden in special lineages in which only those most qualified and sincere were able to learn. With each generation, the Gurus would imbue this wisdom with their own experiences, spiritual realizations, and personal flavor, and this wisdom of Veda became sweeter, thicker, and more applicable.

Many of the great kings of the East studied the knowledge of Veda, and with it, they not only lived peaceful and purposeful lives that progressed to enlightenment, they also effectively created and managed legendary empires.

We are fortunate to have access to this vast and profound body of knowledge, which until now has been unavailable to most of the world. We have seen little bits of this knowledge surface in the Western world and it is beautiful to see that even fragments of this complete knowledge system has transformed the lives of so many. Yoga is a good example. It is only one small portion of the vast Vedic wisdom (about 5 percent), yet people can immediately feel its power and benefits. Just imagine how knowing and applying 100 percent of this complete wisdom system could help you.

> **Contemplation:** Take a moment and imagine yourself having the superpower of knowing exactly how and what to do in any situation to create the results you wanted. Ask yourself what you would create with such power.

Veda = Knowledge

The word *Veda* means "knowledge," but when it's used, it generally refers to a vast body of literature that was written at least 5,000 to 7,000 years ago. This compilation of Vedic texts is several libraries large and the wisdom contained within them is considered by the residents of the East, such as India, Nepal, Bali, and Tibet, to be far older than 7,000 years. Linguistically when I write *Veda* or *Vedas,* I am referring to the knowledge within this vast library of books. When I say *Vedic,* it means "from the Vedas" or "of the Vedas" (for example, Vedic wisdom, Vedic practice, Vedic meditation, Vedic knowledge).

The Vedas were written as captivating hymns, poems, and prayers. Originally disciples would learn the Vedas from their guru teachers by memorizing the verses. When I was a young monk in the monastery we also memorized many of these sweet hymns (mantras) of the Vedas. To this day, reciting these verses brings me peace and solace.

An Eternal Principle

The concept of Veda goes way beyond that of mystical poetry and 5,000-year-old wisdom. Veda is understood by the scholars and spiritual practitioners of the East to be the eternal knowledge that constantly pulsates through all of existence.

When someone is spiritually attuned they are able to tap into this eternal knowledge of Veda. This type of realized knowledge is what we aim for when trying to be fully effective and progress to passionate enlightenment.

Of course, being able to do this constantly and consistently is a sign of being extremely spiritually exalted. Yet still, through simply attempting to surrender spiritually (a concept we will explore shortly), you can connect with this eternal knowledge of Veda.

Enlightened beings are fully realized in Veda and connect with it all the time. They do not need to read books or memorize any verses; all the knowledge of the universe is accessible to them. All they need to do is to enter into meditation, and any information they need appears in their heart.

To make the spiritual process easier for those of us who are not fully enlightened, enlightened souls have tapped into this eternal pulsating wisdom and written it down in the form of the Vedic texts.

Some call this process of tuning into the eternal wisdom of Veda "channeling," some say it is an internal inspiration, and some go as far as saying its God telling them what to write. Almost every spiritual lineage and almost every religion has some form of a Guru, profit, or teacher channeling divine knowledge and either speaking it as a lecture or documenting it as a book to assist us less-advanced souls. I believe that classic spiritual texts such as the Bible and Torah are all results of such enlightened channeling. Of course there are many phony "Gurus" and "prophets" who are either deluded or deceitful that say they do this.

The Vedas Teach Every Facet of Existence

The Vedas do not solely focus on only one part of life. They give detailed knowledge on pretty much every aspect of it. Actually, they don't just teach about every aspect of life, they teach about every facet of existence. Basically, everything in the universe is discussed in the Vedas. There are libraries full of Vedic texts for every subject imaginable. A few examples: wealth, music meditation, sex (yes, the Kama Sutra is part of Vedic knowledge), liberation, health, spirituality, war, politics, God, mysticism, architecture, relationships, love, mathematics, agriculture, astrology, astronomy, and so much more!

All the wisdom of the Vedas slowly but surely guides us toward enlightenment. They don't see enlightenment as just another facet of life, but the purpose, the end goal, and the highest perfection of life.

Though much more satisfying than any material attainment, such as making money or a passionate relationship, enlightenment is most easily attained when approached in the context of the rest of life. Therefore, the Vedas, which are ultimately a deep thesis and guide to enlightenment, empower us in all parts of our life.

In this training we will learn a simple but profound framework that is both derived from the Vedas yet still new. We will learn how reality works and how to be effective in it. I am starting this book with a bit of theory, but this book is a practical one: The Unprecedented Elemental Reality System provided herein will empower you to be effective in everything you do, and it will guide you in attaining the most beautiful and ever-sweet passionate enlightenment.

> **Contemplation:** Take a moment and contemplate how doing better in the practical parts of your life, such as in business and relationships, could help your spiritual growth. Then contemplate how growing spiritually may also help your practical life.

Realized vs. Theoretical Knowledge

Realized knowledge is different from information or theory. Information is just data, whereas realized knowledge, which is often known as wisdom, is knowledge that, in a sense, becomes part of who you are. Realized knowledge is always accessible and there to help you in every moment and in every action, whereas theoretical knowledge may not be used practically. Realized knowledge is active; theoretical knowledge is passive. Knowledge is only realized knowledge when it is used or experienced.

For example, knowledge in a cookbook is theoretical. Just because someone reads a cookbook does not mean that they now know how to cook. The ability to actually cook without a cookbook is realized knowledge, whereas the data written in the cookbook is just theoretical information. As another example, think about a mango. One person may know the chemical composition of a mango but never tasted one. Their knowledge is theoretical. Another person may eat a mango and thus know how it tastes and feel the nourishment from it. This is realized knowledge.

I want you to be able to taste the sweet mango of enlightenment. Throughout this book I give you practices, exercises, and subjects to contemplate that will help you to assimilate what you are learning and integrate it into the core of your being so that it stays with you and helps you forever.

> If I were to speak with another senior monk and tell them what this book was about, I would say, "I am teaching people how to find their Eternal Dharma and showing them what to do so that they can manifest it, while at the same time showing them how to use the ancient wisdom of Veda to be extraordinarily effective in their life."

The Principle of Dharma

Yay! We get to explore one of my favorite and also one of the most misunderstood principles of the East: the principle of *dharma*.

The principle of dharma is the foundation of 5,000-year-old Vedic wisdom of India of which this book is a representation. Knowing this principle and how to apply it in your life is one of the most powerful things that you can do. Knowing the principle of dharma is paramount if you want to understand pretty much anything, or be effective in getting anything that you want. I found this principle to be so important that I chose it as the main focus of my PhD thesis.

By the end of the next two chapters, you should have a clear understanding of what dharma is, as well as a clearer recognition of the profundity of Spiritual Surrender as your highest Eternal Dharma.

You may have heard the word *dharma* before. It is a word in the archaic Indian language of Sanskrit and it is gaining popularity in the Western world. However, the concept of dharma is still largely misunderstood. Most people in the East, where the word has been incorporated into the local languages, still don't understand the meaning of dharma.

Some people translate dharma as duty, righteousness, religion, or moral-ity. These translations are okay, but miss the power, depth, intrigue, and use of the word and concept. More accurate meanings of dharma would be inherent function, constitutional nature, sustaining truth, or proclivity. I actually don't believe that there is a single English word or phrase that can properly convey the intricacies of this fine principle.

A General Synopsis of Dharma

Everything in reality, every object in the universe, anything or anyone that exists, has an inherent function, a constitutional nature, a purpose, a truth and tendency that defines its very existence. This nature or inher-ent function is what makes the object or thing be what it is. It is not possible for anything to exist without having such a nature. It is pos-sible for some things to be engaged against their nature, but their inher-ent, built-in nature still remains fixed and is always there. This built-in, inherent constitutional nature is called dharma. Throughout this book, I use the word *dharma* and the phrases *inherent nature* and *inherent function* interchangeably.

The dharma of any given thing is inseparable from that thing; it was, is, and always will be there. The dharma of the object was created at the same time the object was created and will exist as long as the object exists.

Let's look at a few examples to get a clearer understanding of this principle.

A pen has an inherent function, or dharma; it was created for a specific purpose and it has a defining function that makes it a pen. The nature, or function, of a pen is to be written with; that is its dharma. It was created for that, and if it was not created for the purpose of writing and did not have the functional ability to be written with, it would not be a pen: It would be something else.

In the same way, all things have a dharma. The function of a car is to transport; a house, to be lived in; a guitar, for music; a blanket, to keep you warm; food, to nourish; a phone, for communicating—you get the idea. Everything exists to do something.

Everyone and Everything Has a Dharma

It's easy for us to understand this notion of dharma when we look at man-made objects like pens, cars, books, houses, clothes, and so forth. But the true beauty of the concept begins to shine when we see that all things, both inanimate and living, have a dharma. This means that all persons, all objects, all organizations, all eight elements the universe is composed of (described Part 2), and all things in nature, such as plants and animals (basically everything in existence), have a dharma, an inherent constitutional nature.

> **Contemplation:** Look at objects located near you and try to see what their dharma is. Example: pen = to be written with, mouse = to point and click on a computer screen, wall = to hold a ceiling and provide privacy.

Oftentimes when I explain this principle of dharma people ask me what their own dharma is. Though the quick answer to this question is Spiritual Surrender, the truth is, discovering your dharma is no light thing. Each person has an individual and unique personal dharma. Knowing your dharma, your true constitutional nature, is fundamentally important for any type of lasting joy or success in life. Knowing your dharma is the first progression in the evolution of your spiritual journey to enlightenment. The sad fact is that most people do not know their dharma. This means that they don't really know who they are and why they exist. Some people may have a vague idea, but a person who truly knows their dharma is a rare one. If, by the end of reading this book, knowing your dharma was the one and only thing you got from it, I would be happy and satisfied; I would consider my duty as a teacher accomplished. I would know that your life would be at peace, prosperity would flow fully, and you would be well on your way to full Passionate Enlightenment. I would need not have any more worries for you, my friend. Still, because, as human beings, we have an enormous capacity to learn and grow, I am filling this book with many more tools and principles; this principle of dharma is just the beginning.

Let's continue to look at the principle of dharma from several more perspectives, so you can get a deeper, more complete understanding of it.

Dharma as Inherent Nature

I think that perhaps the best definition of the word *dharma* is "inherent nature." Everything has a nature and the nature of any given thing is automatically there. Rarely would we ask where this inherent nature comes from; it's just there. It is built-in and automatic and takes no extra effort to exist. Using things in alignment with their inherent nature also takes little to no effort. Things want to be as they naturally are. Pain and problems come by inhibiting nature, but rarely is there a problem when we let things just be as they naturally are. There can be no problems caused by living your dharma or by letting others live theirs.

Attempting to Dominate Nature

Society often tries to restrict, dominate, and control nature; it often succeeds, but only temporarily. Such curving and curtailing of inherent nature can only be sustained for a short period of time—and that period is troublesome and often outright hurtful. One example of this is authoritarian governmental regimes, like dictatorships, that deny or try to reshape human nature. These regimes have a short life span. Eventually they crumble, as anything that tries to repress nature must. We cannot successfully dominate over nature and we cannot actually curtail it to act according to our will. All we can do is align ourselves with it and trust in perfectness.

A good visual of this is an old stone wall in the forest. For some time it kept nature in check, but now plants and insects have dug in and made their homes there. Grass grows in its cracks, and a tree has rooted itself there. The once-almighty wall is now crumbling, and in a few more years it will be reduced to rubble or even disintegrate completely. Nature is the mightiest; and although the conditioned ego strives to triumph over nature, it cannot. That is the simple truth.

A Smarter Strategy

A smarter strategy, other than trying to artificially dominate over the inherent nature of things, is to strategically use the principle of dharma. This means to understand one's own dharma and the dharma of the environment (other objects or persons in the equation), and then act in such a way that is in natural harmony with all those dharmas. Doing this allows you to create long-lasting, superior quality results with much less effort. Plus, acting in accordance with dharma is a much more joyful experience.

> **Contemplation:** Think of at least three places or times in your life where you tried to go against nature. You wanted to control things and make them be something they were not. What were the results of such actions? Two of my experiences of this were trying to have my assistants do things that were against their inherent core nature and trying to use a salad bowl to cook.

Dharma as the Defining Quality

Dharma can also be seen as the defining qualities of an object. Take water, for example. What makes water, water? Water has certain qualities that make it water, such as wetness, fluidity, and the ability to take the shape of its container. As long as water retains these qualities, it can be called water. The dharma of water is its inherent and natural qualities. These qualities are inseparable and define what a given object or thing is.

Dharma as a Constitution

Dharma is like the constitution or set of rules that govern an object. Just like the constitution of a nation is the very foundation and bedrock of how it operates, and the rules of the constitution prevail and govern that nation, the rules of dharma prevail and govern any given object, individual, or organization.

The rules of dharma are inherent and natural; they are not imposed from any external source. They constitutionally live in the very DNA of an object, so to speak. Fire, for example, has a dharma that is to shine, heat, and light. If there was a law that governed fire, it would be something to the effect of "Thou shalt shine, heat, and give light." This requires no change from the fire because that is what fire is and does: It shines, heats, and gives light.

In the same way, your dharma is your constitution—your own personal set of rules. It is what you do and what you don't do, who you are and who you are not. Many self-help "gurus" will have you write a personal constitution or manifesto. They will tell you to decide who you want to be and then write your own manifesto according to the vision you invented for yourself. The exercises they prescribe are useful and have helped many people, but a superior approach would be to learn how to find and uncover what your inherent constitutional dharma is. A personal constitution code that is a reflection and expression of your inner constitutional nature, your dharma, is far superior to any form of trying to invent what you think it should be or adopting rules imposed from an external source. (At the end of the next chapter I will give you an exercise to help you craft your Personal Dharma Code as a guide to help you live your life with purpose, in passionate-loving-spiritual connection and in your maximum power. I will also give you some tips on how to set up your life in order to support the further uncovering of your dharma.)

Dharma as a Proclivity

Because one's dharma is one's natural state, there is a natural tendency, inclination, or proclivity, to go toward doing one's dharma. Water naturally will revert to being wet and fluid whenever it can, because being wet and fluid is the dharma of water. Being frozen and hard like ice is unnatural for water and is not its dharma. This means that you are naturally attracted to doing your dharma. It is an easy and natural expression of your beautiful self to live in dharma.

Though each individual's dharma is personal and unique, part of the core dharma of all living beings is to connect in love. Therefore, everyone naturally wants and has a proclivity to move toward love and connection. The subject of love and connection is the crux and core truth of life, the universe, and everything in existence. All true wisdom is there to lead us to divine transcendental, spiritual loving union, which is known as and attained by Spiritual Surrender. In later chapters of this book we will delve into uncovering the lush, living, lustful, licentious, ludicrousness of love.

> **Contemplation:** Write down at least three possibilities of what your core dharma might be. It may take weeks, months, or even years to figure out what your core dharma is; this is normal. For now, just do this exercise to get your brain contemplating this vital subject.

Dharma as Duty

Another part of the concept of dharma is that dharma is duty. You have an obligation to execute your dharma. You must do what you are meant to do. You must be what you are meant to be. This is not just a duty to yourself: We, the other people on this planet, need you to shine bright and live in your fullest expression of love, your dharma. Do not hide your gifts from us!

Living life in accordance to your dharma is both the most selfish and most selfless thing you can do. Often in spiritual circles there is too much emphasis put on "being" and too little emphasis put on "doing." This is laziness, selfishness, and often born from a misconception of the spiritual. Action is vital for life. Dharma includes action. A pen must be written with, water must flow, and conscious beings must love. We as living beings must act.

Enlightened action is action that is done in accordance with dharma and is a necessity when walking the path to enlightenment.

Dharma as Religion

People often translate dharma as religion. Though there is much beauty and spiritual connection in most or all of the world's religions, this is my least-favorite translation of the word. The history of religious institutions using ideology and dogma to manipulate and control people, and the number of wars that have been started and fueled by religion, are just too much. How many people have been killed in the name of God? I feel religious fanaticism is just too rampant to translate dharma as religion.

I see why dharma is translated as religion, though. The true purpose of religion is to guide us in perfect action so that we can connect with the divine, or, as some would say, God. Dharma also does this. When one is enlightened they are living in their fullest dharma. When one has not yet become fully enlightened it is hard for them to always know their dharma. Therefore, saints of the past have given spiritual instructions and guidelines to help people on their spiritual path. These instructions have turned into religions. Most of the original instructions themselves are pure and beautiful, but oftentimes, as time passes, people distort them. Therefore, in the true, unadulterated sense of religion, religion is dharma. True religion is meant to lead us to manifesting our dharma.

It is important to know that Indian languages use the word *dharma* to mean religion. Very few people have as much of an in-depth understanding of the concept of dharma as you now have.

Dharma Is Happiness

Happiness, inner contentment, peace, and passionate loving connection come naturally when you act in accordance to your dharma. Being happy is part of the core dharma of all living beings. For example, a fish's dharma is to be in water, and when it is in water it is happy and it is peaceful. When you take it out of water, it cannot be happy no matter what you supply it with. Give him an unlimited supply of premium-brand fish food, an entire harem of flamboyant female fish, and an oversized television, yet he will still not be happy. The fish, like everyone, needs to act in accordance to his dharma to be happy. He needs water.

Another example: Water cannot be happy when it goes against its dharma and exists as steam. It always strives to condense and become water again.

In the same way, you cannot be happy unless you are living your fullest spiritual potential, your dharma. Living your dharma is the only cause of sustainable and everlasting contentment, happiness, and joy. Your dharma is who you are. Your dharma is your purpose.

Dharma the Sustaining Truth

Dharma can be called the sustaining truth of a person or thing. This concept can be a bit of a mind twist, but it is really fun when you understand it. Words in the Sanskrit language originate in shorter words known as *verbal roots*. By going into the meaning of these verbal roots you get a better understanding of the word. The verbal root of dharma is *dhri*. The literal meaning for the verbal root *dhri* is to hold, to sustain, to bear, to carry, to maintain. In this context this means that dharma is the very sustaining and maintaining principle that holds any item together. An item would not exist if it had no dharma. An item is able to exist simply because of its dharma. In our previous example of a pen we saw how a pen is not a pen if it does not write and its creation was not intended for writing. If a pen has no dharma, it is not a pen.

In order to see this principle in action, let's use a business as an example. Let's say the business is a mobile phone company. So, its dharma is to provide its customers with mobile phones. If it sells potatoes instead, or just gets caught up in corporate bureaucracy and stops giving customers mobile phones, it will either go out of business or no longer be a mobile phone company. The mobile phone company will not hold together, it will not be sustained, and eventually it will cease to exist.

Food is the same way. Is food indeed food if it is not edible? Is a business a business if it makes no money and provides no services? Is a marriage a marriage if there is no love, connection, and cohabitation? Is a human being a human being if he or she does not think and does not love? Dharma allows for existence: no dharma = no existence.

On the other side, the more energy we put toward executing dharma, the higher quality of existence we can have. The more a business focuses on dharma, the more it will grow; the more a couple focuses on their dharma, the more their relationship will flourish. The more we focus on our Eternal Dharma, the more spiritually connected and happy we will be.

My friend, congratulations! You have completed the first chapter. That was quite intellectual, so good job! Spiritual growth and effective action are practices by nature. Therefore even though we are just getting started with the foundational principals and have not yet started gearing up for focused action, here is a meditation exercise I advise you to start practicing. It will help the intellectual stuff digest and gradually supply you with a whole host of benefits that will become clear as you practice and read the rest of this book.

The "Gopal" Exercise

Sound vibration is powerful. Sound exists in all things. One of the most significant ancient spiritual practices is mantra meditation. In order to calm your mind and enlighten your inner self, I suggest you begin by starting with the simple practice outlined here. This exercise has a lot of explanation, meaning, and power, which we will explore in-depth in later chapters. Just as you don't need to know the recipe to eat good food, you can reap the benefits of peace, power, connection, and universal alignment from this exercise before we explore how it works.

Do this daily. Though any time will work, I suggest you do this exercise after you shower in the morning and before you go to bed.

Step 1: Find a quiet place.

Step 2: Sit in a comfortable position.

Step 3: Set a timer for 8 minutes. (Any smartphone should have an app with a timer; turn off notifications.)

Step 4: Fold your hands and hold them at chest level.

Step 5: Bring awareness to your breath, and breathe deeply.

Step 4: Repeat the mantra "Gopal" three times every time you breathe out.

CHAPTER 2

FINDING YOUR DHARMA

 Not all dharmas are created equal. There are two types of dharmas:

1. Eternal Dharma. The real dharma that is inherent and inseparable from the person or object.
2. Temporary Dharma: A dharma that is taken on at a specific time and is caused by the influence of circumstances and environment.

Eternal Dharma

It is only possible to understand Eternal Dharma if we first understand that some things are eternal. Ancient spiritual wisdom teaches us that we are eternal. Our body and mind are always going through changes, but the one thing that remains constant is us. Every seven years, every cell of our body changes; our mind also changes drastically as we grow from being a baby to being elderly. We are the eternal being that exists beyond this body and mind. For a temporary time we inhabit this human body.

Just like we inhabited a child's body for some time, we thought it was us: We thought we were that child's body, but now we have matured. We have evolved past that body. We no longer identify with the child's body; it no longer exists, but we still do exist. In the same way, we will evolve and mature past our current body into a different body. The 5,000-year-old Vedic wisdom of India says that this process of evolving into a new body does not stop at death. It says we are eternal beings.

The subject matter of who we are beyond the body as eternal beings is beautiful and extremely important. In Chapter 13 we will explore this in depth. At this point, all you need to know is that there is one type of dharma that is eternal, and just like you, it always existed and always will exist.

This simplest way of understanding both Eternal Dharma and Temporary Dharma is to know that each of us is a spirit-soul, an eternal living being beyond this body who always strives for happiness and love. For some to-be-explored-later reasons, we have been born into a body that we identify with. The soul has one dharma; the body has another. The dharma of the soul is eternal; the dharma of the body is temporary. The dharma of the soul never changes; the dharma of the body changes according to its context such as age, societal role, gender, karma (which can be translated as both actions and reactions), and so forth.

Our Temporary Dharmas

Water may be put in a freezer and apparently lose the natural qualities and tendencies that make up its dharma. When it becomes ice it becomes hard, it will not take the shape of its container, and it is no longer fluid. It seems to have changed its dharma but it has not; it has simply acquired a temporary nature—a Temporary Dharma. The dharma of water, which is to be wet and fluid, is still there, but it is there as a latent, hidden potential. When the water is taken out of the freezer it reverts back to its natural state—its true dharma. The temporary nature of being ice was acquired by the influence of an unnatural situation or environment.

It is possible for something to be put in an unnatural situation for a long-enough period in which it will appear that the Temporary Dharma, acquired from the influence of the unnatural situation, is its real dharma. Water that is frozen in the North Pole may spend more time as ice, acting according to its acquired Temporary Dharma, than it will as fluid and wet water. It may seem that its real dharma is to be cold and hard like ice. But regardless of what it seems, the dharma of water is to be fluid and wet. Eternal Dharma can only be hidden and can never be destroyed.

All dharmas pertaining to, depending on, and related with our bodies and minds are temporary because our bodies and minds are temporary. Misidentifying with the body and mind begins to freeze the dharma of the soul. The dharma of the soul is selfless love; the frozen acquired Temporary Dharma of the soul is selfishness and is pervaded by negative qualities such as lust, anger, greed, and envy. By surrendering spiritually we can start to identify with our true self—with who we are as spirit-souls. We will no longer misidentify with the body and mind, and thus the ice of our temporary, materially conditioned dharma will begin to melt, situating us in our unadulterated purest state of love.

2 Types of Temporary Dharma

1. HARMFUL TEMPORARY DHARMA

A Harmful Temporary Dharma is a tendency or proclivity that is acquired due to unhealthy influences. This concept, just like all Vedic concepts, can be applied in many circumstances, but the core and most prominent Harmful Temporary Dharma is when we identify with this body and mind, thus causing the Eternal Dharma of the soul to become dormant.

A good example of a Harmful Temporary Dharma would be of a drunkard. It seems that his dharma is to drink alcohol and be intoxicated because he has a tendency toward doing this. But we all know that it's not his natural state of being. This is an acquired Harmful Temporary Dharma. By going through rehab, the ice-like Harmful Temporary Dharma will melt, and he will revert back to his original state of sobriety.

We all have many such acquired Harmful Temporary Dharmas, but the truth is I don't have the time and space in this book to go into depth on this point (actually on many points: The Vedic wisdom is simply too vast).

2. Beneficial Temporary Dharma

There is also a type of Temporary Dharma that is beneficial. Acting according to it helps you to be peaceful and effective. Following your Beneficial Temporary Dharma also helps you on your path to Passionate Enlightenment.

A Beneficial Temporary Dharma is basically the dharma of the body and mind. Because all things have a dharma, the body and mind also have a dharma. By identifying with the body and mind you adopt the dharma of the body and mind. Beneficial Temporary Dharmas are one's duties, responsibilities, tendencies, skills, careers, special gifts, and capabilities. Your worldly designations, such as relationships and societal roles, also play a part in creating your Beneficial Temporary Dharma.

Temporary Dharmas cannot, do not, and will never compare with Eternal Dharma because they are born from the temporary body and mind. Temporary Dharmas cannot, however, be denied. Our body is the vehicle we use to advance to an enlightened connection with the divine. Therefore, by following Beneficial Temporary Dharmas our consciousness gradually becomes elevated, which makes it possible to eventually operate from our Eternal Dharma. Following Temporary Dharma slowly helps us transcend beyond the body. We may start by operating 95 percent from our Temporary Dharma and 5 percent from our Eternal Dharma. As we advance, this ratio will change until we are operating 100 percent from our Eternal Dharma, which is the point when we are fully enlightened. Though Eternal Dharma takes prominence over Temporary Dharma, it is beneficial and essential to execute both of our dharmas simultaneously.

A good example of a Beneficial Temporary Dharma based on the body is that of a mother. Once her baby is born it is her dharma, her duty, her nature, to nurture her baby. This dharma is temporary; it never existed before. And as the baby grows up the duty of the mother will change; her dharma will change. Yet it is crucial for her to execute her Beneficial Temporary Dharma; she will be happier by doing it and the world will be a better place for it. In executing her Beneficial Temporary Dharma, she will cultivate selflessness and other qualities that are a good foundation for proceeding to enlightenment.

Other examples of Beneficial Temporary Dharmas are: spouse, teacher, student, officer, parent, son, daughter, boyfriend, girlfriend, business executive, farmer, secretary, sibling, pilot, actor, fireman, model, scientist, athlete, politician, activist, and so forth. There are millions Beneficial Temporary Dharmas; pretty much every career, role, or duty can be a Beneficial Temporary Dharma.

The question is often "How do I find my Beneficial Temporary Dharma?" I have included an exercise at the end of this chapter to help you pinpoint your Beneficial Temporary Dharma.

It is important to know that, though Beneficial Temporary Dharmas are acquired and may be flexible according to time, place, and circumstance, they are, in a way, also inherent and fixed. They come along with our body, mind, and life situations; therefore, as long as body, mind, and the life situations exist, their corresponding Beneficial Temporary Dharmas will exist.

Where this Dharma comes from is another large subject. It is the subject of what determines our birth, our tendencies, desires, and gifts. Later on in this book, this should also become clear. For now all we need to know is that each person has an individual Beneficial Temporary Dharma—gift, duty—that, when properly executed, will grant them the most happiness and would serve the world in the best way possible.

Exercise 1: Finding your Dharma

This exercise is meant to help you find your Core Beneficial Temporary Dharma. Uncovering your fullest and highest spiritual Eternal Dharma is what spiritual life is, and it will only be fully revealed once you are fully enlightened.

Go through the process of this exercise on paper or at a computer. Don't skip ahead; only look at the next question once you have finished the previous question, though it may seem strange to do this.

Time: 30 to 60 minutes

Part 1

Step 1: Look around the room or wherever you are.

Step 2: Pick out two objects.

Step 3: Write down the dharma of each of the objects.

Here are some questions to help you in this process. What was it made for? What does it do best? What is the one thing that if it did would be enough? What is the one thing that if it did not do, would not be okay? How long has it done that for? What is natural for it?

Step 4: Envision using that object perfectly according to its dharma. Try to measure or envision the results.

Step 5: Envision using that object completely against its dharma. Try to measure or envision the results.

Step 6: Write the dharma of the following things: a brick, a potato, a policeman, a taxi driver, a CEO, a mother. (You may use the questions above to help you.)

Part 2

Step 1: Answer the following question in four sentences or less. Take no more than seven minutes to answer this question. (You may use the questions from Step 3 in Part 1 of this exercise to help you.)

What is your dharma?

Step 2: Answer the following questions:

What do you love to do?
What do you do best?
What actions come easily and naturally to you?
What do others appreciate about you?
When do you feel the happiest?
What actions (of service) bring you the most joy and happiness?
What is the greatest contribution you can make?
When do you thrive?
What mission scares you deeply?

What would you like to be when you grow up?

What role do you play in society?

What role do you play for your family?

Think of a time when you effortlessly helped someone but yet it touched them in a profoundly way. How did you serve them?

What are your dreams and aspirations?

What were you born to do?

What is your dharma?

Step 3: Go about your day and contemplate your dharma. Have a good night's rest, then, in the morning, spend a few minutes writing what your Beneficial Temporary Dharma is.

Following are notes for those who, after completing this exercise, are still not clear on what their Beneficial Temporary Dharma is:

- I suggest doing this exercise several times. For some people it is best to visit this exercise again in a week or two.

- Your dharma may not be in the form of a mission or career, it could be as soft and beautiful as loving and sweetly caring for your family or radiantly sharing your beauty or art.

- Your dharma is always in service. It's about contribution and giving. It is hard to see your dharma when your attention is on yourself, your problems, and your desires. The more selfless we are, the easier it is to clearly see our dharma. A good practice to is to intentionally be more selfless for sets periods of time—consciously choosing to give your love, energy, and attention to others. You can do this by doing things for other people, listening to them, and serving them. This way the selfishness caused by the unnatural conditioning of this world will melt; your Harmful Temporary Dharma will begin to melt, thus making it easier to find your Beneficial Temporary Dharma. Then, by following your Beneficial Temporary Dharma, your Harmful Temporary Dharma will continue to melt more, making it easier to engage in Spiritual Surrender.

- We all have multiple Temporary Dharmas. Your Beneficial Temporary Dharma may not be clear in the beginning because you may have a few of them.
- Yet another thing to keep in mind is that knowing yourself takes time. Discovering your dharma can take years, so do not lose heart if things are not clear yet. I have faith in you; you are on the right path. What your Beneficial Temporary Dharma is and what your Eternal Dharma is will all become clear in time.

Pain, disease, and lack of efficacy are caused when you go against dharma. There is a disharmony in any action that is not done in dharma. A musical instrument played out of harmony with the orchestra gives no pleasure. A finger bent the wrong way hurts. A phone used as a hammer yields ineffective results.

According to the Vedic concept of dharma, if something is going against its dharma it cannot be peaceful. It cannot be happy. It will only cause pain and turmoil. Therefore, the first lesson in powerful living is to seek out one's own dharma and know the dharma of whatever and whoever one may be working with.

This is a spiritual book, and therefore I must tell you that the highest understanding of the concept of dharma is in Eternal Dharma. Throughout this book we will dive deeply into the practical application of Beneficial Temporary Dharma, we will dive deeply into how to use this and other principles for Effective Action and personal gain and we will dive deeper into the spiritual domain. But always keep in mind, my friend, that the highest Eternal Dharma is a passionate, spiritual, loving connection with the divine. By nature we are all individuals and, therefore, we all have an individual unique relationship with the divine. We all have an individual, personal, and unique dharma.

Dharma Alignment for Success

There is no such thing as success without dharma. Stalin accomplished many things, but he could not be fulfilled and happy, and his effectiveness was limited. Even though he commanded great power, enough to change and create history, his actions were contrary to dharma. He had a whole nation go against dharma. So, even though he accomplished great feats such as conquering other nations, influencing and (mis)leading, as well as killing millions of people, it would have been impossible for him to have effective sustainable results in his endeavors. Going against dharma is like bending your finger the wrong way. You can stretch it a lot and become good at bending your finger backward, but you will never be able to use it with the same effectiveness as bending your fingers forward and using your hand according to its dharma—the way it was meant to be used. Stalin had an entire nation going against dharma, so it was only a matter of time before his regime crumbled.

Don't build a business on the wrong foundation; don't do any project or have any goal in life that goes against your dharma or the dharma of the people and things involved. It will fail and you will not be satisfied. It will harm the world. The most effective venture is one that is most aligned with your dharma and the dharma of everyone and everything involved. Everyone is allowed and facilitated to act in their fullest. If every person involved in the project is working according to their dharma, then they will be the most productive and garner the greatest results.

The Beauty of Purpose and Universal Alignment

With this vision, a special beauty in the world, the universe, and the whole cosmic manifestation begins to emerge. Now, all of a sudden, everything has purpose and meaning. A rock, a tree, or a waterfall does not simply exist: It exists with dharma. There is a reason for that rock to be. You may not know it yet, but as you ascend the path to enlightenment that inner knowing—that realized knowledge—begins to come forth and you can know the dharma of a rock, a tree, or anything. But why? Why does it matter to know the dharma of a rock? By seeing the rock as meaningful— as having purpose—it changes your relationship with it. This kind of vision changes your relationship with all of reality and with life. You can not only use that knowledge for effectiveness, but a spiritual awareness begins to emerge, and the world becomes magical. You begin to sense a cosmic consciousness in all things. You begin to feel that everything is part of a divine order, a divine plan. You understand that all of reality is working perfectly beyond your control; so, you are free to bask in the sweet serenity of Spiritual Surrender—for everything exists in perfect harmony and alignment.

The beauty of seeing all of life, purpose, and dharma within a rock stems from another one of my favorite concepts: Universal Alignment. This idea says that everything in existence functions in a divine harmony. Everything in the universe has its place and has a dharma. The universe is like clockwork: Every part has its role and is interdependent, interconnected, and inter-supportive of every other part. The whole universe works in harmony.

The planets and galaxies move in their orbits in perfect unison. The sun provides heat, light, and nourishment, without which there would be no life on earth. But with perfect precision the earth spins at a thousand miles per hour and moves ever so slightly in its orbit to not only make a perfect habitat for life, but also to give us different seasons. Every morning the sun rises and sets in perfect timing. I find contemplating the cosmic harmony of existence extraordinarily fascinatingly amazing. Every time I do it my chest flutters in awe of the sheer magnitude and beauty of the Universe. Just think about oxygen: We breathe out what plants breathe in, and they breathe in what we breathe out. Just think of the magnetic pull of the moon that influences bodies of water with such precision that we can have tides and waves to surf but still build our homes by the beach. Plants grow us food, we eat it, and our wastage is now food for plants. Just think of ecosystems. Food grows by bees pollinating plants. This world is amazing. We are in such a symbiotic relationship with existence that it is mind-boggling to perceive. I can go on and on explaining the amazing harmony of existence. But I think you understand. There is a natural unison, harmony, and alignment in the universe.

When we combine this concept of Universal Alignment with the concept of dharma we can see that all things have their place in the universe. It is almost as if life, reality, and existence are like a giant orchestra: Each instrument has an important part to play in the musical masterpiece, and the result is beauty extraordinaire. When things function according to dharma, they are automatically in harmony with all other things in existence.

Exercise 2: Crafting your Personal Dharma Code

You may want to write your Personal Dharma Code. It is a highly beneficial exercise, and some people love to keep this code as their personal manifesto—a sort of rulebook that they live their life by.

Life is ultimately more fluid than what can be captured by any set of rules, and I prefer that you are guided by the natural expression of who you are, rather than by a set of rules. In any case, a Personal Dharma Code can be extremely helpful. Here is how you do it.

Step 1: Write your Eternal Dharma on the top of a fresh sheet of paper (or in a new digital document). At this point I suggest you write Spiritual Surrender or Passionate Enlightenment.

Step 2: Write a list of your Core Beneficial Temporary Dharmas. (If you are unclear on what that is, repeat Exercise 1: Finding Your Dharma.) For this exercise I suggest you condense the description of your Core Beneficial Temporary Dharma to one sentence or phrase if you have not done so yet.

Step 3: Create and write down three to eight laws that are an expression of your Core Beneficial Temporary Dharma.

Example: Core Beneficial Temporary Dharma = nourish my family with my love, care, and cooking

Law 1: I always put my heart into my cooking.

Law 2: I always strive to give empathy and sensitively; I listen to the feelings of those I love.

Law 3: I let no hardness enter my heart.

Dharma in Business

The ideal business is one whose dharma is clear. Everybody in the company knows the dharma of the business and acts to fulfill that dharma. Each person working in the company does not have to bend out of his or her dharma to fulfill the dharma of the business. Each individual dharma flourishes fully and naturally, and by doing so they are doing the best thing possible for the business: Salespeople sell, organizers organize, creators create, and so forth.

You will probably have to restructure your business and do some hiring and firing. It may seem harsh to fire some people, especially when it is your dharma to provide jobs, but by doing so you will be doing the person, your company, and your sanity a favor. No one will be happy, effective, or living their higher purpose if they are employed contrarily to their dharma.

Quick Tips

1. Check to make sure that what you are doing is in alignment with your dharma. If it is, persevere at all costs; if it is not, then stop doing it. Only do your dharma.

   When things are tough and difficult in life, you may need to persevere. Life is not always meant to be easy. There is virtue in pushing through. But be careful: Do not waste time and energy on things that are not your dharma.

2. When you are trying to do something with a machine or tool and it is just not working, check to make sure that you are using the tool according to its dharma. Ask yourself: "Was the machine, software, or device made to be used in that way?" Is it meant to do what you are trying to get it to do? If it is, is it meant to do it in the way you are doing it?

Congratulations! These have been an intense two chapters in which we uncovered many deep truths and did some powerful intellectual gymnastics. I am impressed that you made it this far and applaud you for your tenacity. Now you know more about dharma than most people on planet Earth; you even know more than many monks and spiritual teachers.

In Chapter 3, we will explore three other, less-technical foundational concepts before we start the main course of this book: the Unprecedented Elemental Reality System.

Spiritual Surrender and Integration

 My friend, I strongly, confidently, and emphatically declare two things:

1. Spiritual Surrender is the most important and essential key to spiritual growth.
2. Spiritual Surrender is the most effective way to operate for power and success.

Spiritual Surrender: The Most Essential Key to Spiritual Growth

This first declaration is perhaps not as radical a claim as the second. Throughout history the earth has been blessed with thousands of spiritual teachers, spread over thousands of traditions, thousands of spiritual books have been written, and millions of speeches have been given. When you look deeply, it is easy to see that all of this has been aimed at helping us progress to this rare and sweet state of Spiritual Surrender. Therefore,

I strongly believe that without being absorbed in the seductive, sublime Spiritual Surrender, we will not be able to actually comprehend, taste, and absorb ourselves in the fathomless beauty of divine existence that all spiritual wisdom wants us to relish.

Spiritual Surrender: The Most Effective Way to Operate for Power and Success

This second declaration is perhaps more controversial and radical. I say that spiritual wisdom is not simply meant to be philosophy, some ambiguous jargon, or blank promises. It is meant to be relished, and used practically in every action and in every millisecond of life.

Many of us strive for effective action. We want every action we take to be successful. We want to produce the maximum results with a minimal amount of effort. We want to remain happy, purposeful, enthused, and uplifted throughout the process. In essence, we want happiness-infused power. Contrary to what many people believe, ancient wisdom shows us that when spiritual wisdom is practiced properly it generates such happiness-infused power.

It is inspiring to understand and therefore I state that such happiness-infused power can only be achieved, in its fullest and perfect sense, through Spiritual Surrender. Think about that. With this declaration I am saying that no business, project, relationship, or military exposition can be fully effective unless the people involved learn and practice the same ancient spiritual principles that are taught and followed by bald-headed monks in funny-looking, flowy robes.

The rest of this book will be not only to back up these statements but will also guide you in how to manifest your deepest loving spiritual potential and how to live with full effective power in this world.

After all this, you may be wondering what Spiritual Surrender is. Spiritual Surrender is a vast concept that can be approached in many ways. Here are several angles so you can get a feel for this deep yet elusive principle.

In a nutshell Spiritual Surrender is when we act according to our inherent function/dharma and thus connect in love with a higher power. We acknowledge that it is not possible for us to do it all alone, and by surrendering to a higher power to guide us, we can make the best decisions, be happy, and be fully empowered.

Another way of understanding the essence of Spiritual Surrender is to see it as the highest and most passionate loving state of enlightenment.

But let's look deeper.

A Loving Connection With the Divine

Spiritual Surrender is an experience of love, connection, and relationship. Spiritual Surrender is the beginning of a divine relationship with the absolute that is beyond the body and mind.

In order to start the process of love in Spiritual Surrender first we must acknowledge that there is a higher power. We must know that there is something or someone that is living and breathing all of life, a power greater than our own that causes everything to exist and function in the universe.

Throughout history this power has been called many names, such as Nature, God, the Universe, the Supersoul, the Supreme Being, and so on. Religions have also approached this incomprehensible one indivisible absolute truth and address It, Him, or Her with many names, such as The Father, Christ, Krishna, Buddha, Allah, and Jehovah. The point here is not to debate which one is "right," for all traditions have their beauty and depth of truth, and work well for the sincere souls who practice in that tradition. Simply understanding that there is some sort of higher power or energy in the Universe is enough to progress on the path of Spiritual Surrender.

The sweetness starts to thicken when we know that this higher power is "a good guy" that is not out to get us, but is actually the source of all beauty, love, and sweetness, and wants to help us. When we choose to accept this help from the divine, we have started on the path of Spiritual Surrender.

In order to accept transcendental help we must not only accept the existence of a higher power, but we must also connect with that power. Love exists in connection and, because Spiritual Surrender is the greatest connection with the divine, it is also the greatest love. The subject of love is the most important subject of life and existence; therefore later chapters of this book will reveal love's hidden mysteries. For now simply know that Spiritual Surrender is an acknowledgment of the existence of a higher power, a loving connection with It, and an acceptance of help from It.

Exercise

Write down three to six times when you felt (or feel) lost and confused, when you knew you needed to do something but you were not clear on what to do. Think of the pain, then think of how relieved you would have been if at that time you had divine guidance that you could trust, leading you to the most perfect action possible.

This may sound unattainable, but it is not. Millions of people worldwide follow such guidance, and I bet there have been times when you have too. The issue is knowing how to recognize such guidance, and receive and follow it on a consistent basis. My friend, it is possible.

Acting According to Your Core Nature

In chapters 1 and 2 we learned that all conscious beings and objects have an inherent core nature—a dharma. Spiritual Surrender is not an external imposition; it is not something unnatural that we must strain do. It is, rather, the natural expression of our core spiritual self; it is our Eternal Dharma. As we advance spiritually and become less covered by limiting conditioning, connection through surrender becomes easier and brings us the unadulterated contentment of the soul. The closer we get to being our pure self, not covered or influenced by the temporary happenings of this world, the more surrendered we will be, for it is the nature of the soul to exist in loving Spiritual Surrender.

Nature functions beautifully, and when it is in charge, there is a natural harmony in existence. Things are only disharmonious and suffer when they step out of alignment with what is natural. Therefore, by surrendering to a higher power, which is the Universe or Nature, we enter into harmony with all of nature and thus the rest of the Universe. When we are in harmony with these things only peace, beauty, love, and efficacy are possible.

Nobody likes seeing false pride. When we see such an ego in someone, it is distasteful and ugly. Thinking that we actually have complete power and control over this material world is simply a misunderstanding. One who is situated in Spiritual Surrender does not have, and thus does not project, a big false ego. They know that the actual doer and cause of all things is a higher force that is beyond their control. People are naturally attracted to them, for they embody both humility and power. Spiritual Surrender is humility in its perfect state.

It takes power to be humble, and I believe that only the strong can do it. Surrendering to a higher spiritual power is the best form of humility because it situates one in their true, powerful identity that is neither artificially inflated nor deflated.

If you swim up-stream it does not usually work very well. There is a natural way in which nature works, and when you align yourself with this, everything you do becomes easier and more effective. Therefore, the trick to maximum effectiveness and the key to the greatest power are to align your efforts with the natural force of nature. From there creating whatever you want is like gently drifting down a stream: It takes little to no strenuous effort. Spiritual Surrender is finding this natural flow and flowing with it.

Now the question is: How do we know what the natural flow of nature is? Figuring this out could be a lifetime process, but luckily we have a short-cut. When we connect with the higher power that is Nature and the source of all existence and let that power guide us, we will be guided to act in accordance with the rest of nature, and thus our actions will be perfect and the most effective possible.

Both a Practice and a Goal

Spiritual Surrender is:

1. **A goal**. Spiritual Surrendering is the transcendental state of being when we are completely pure, not covered by any material conditioning. All lust, anger, greed, selfishness, and envy have left our heart. It is a state when we are perfectly, fully, and completely situated in an unbroken, unwavering,

passionate, loving union with the divine. It is full enlightenment, full self-realization, and fully fledged love in its greatest and most complete form.

2. **A practice and process**. Spiritual Surrender is also the pro-
    cess that leads us to the state of pure Spiritual Surrender
    that I have just described. In every moment of our life and in
    each action we take, we can practice the process of Spiritual
    Surrender and thus advance along the path to enlightenment.
    (Read more about this in Chapter 16.)

In modern-Western-pop spirituality, the idea of being in the present moment—the "now"—has become quite popular. People know that
they should be present in the now but what is still currently not properly
understood in the Western world is what to do when you are present in
the now. People think they need to search for the emptiness in the now
and know that simply by absorbing their consciousness in the now they
can magnify the power of the moment. What most people don't know is
that you can much more than magnify the power of the present moment if
you connect with the divine in that moment.

By connecting with the divine at every moment you are connecting
with the source of everything and will know exactly what the best action
or best thought for the moment is. Even more powerful than being fully
present and connected with the divine in the moment, is when you surrender to do and act according to the will of the divine in that moment. This
way, when surrendering in the moment, you are connecting with the totality of nature and the totality of existence (because the divine is the totality
of existence). Thus harnessing the greatest power, and feeling the greatest
love possible in every micro-second, by letting yourself be guided, you can
do no wrong. Everything you do will be the precisely perfect thing to do.
It would be impossible to calculate such perfect action because you simply cannot get enough information to make such calculations. The divine
does have such information, and knows all things in the past, present, and
future, and out of loving care will guide you in the most perfect way possible. Don't just be present: Be present with love. Don't search for the bland
emptiness of the moment, search for the purpose of every moment.

The Myth of the Spiritual and Material Divide

While traveling on my world tours and meeting people of all walks of life I have observed a common idea that causes people so much distress. This idea says that the spiritual and the material are two separate things. This misconception says that all things in the spiritual domain are of one nature—they are made of one type of thing—whereas the material, the physical, the things of this world that you can see and touch, are essentially made of something different.

The problem with subscribing to this myth is that it inhibits your ability to not only be effective, but to also lead a happy, balanced, healthy, and integrated life.

I have found that there are two types of people or psychologies that lead to the Myth of the Spiritual and Material Divide. I describe them here so that you can see if you have been influenced by these mindsets. If you want every action you take and every experience you live to be the most effective possible and to inundate your being with passionate spiritual bliss, then you must learn how the spiritual and material are integrated and how to act in accordance with their integration. Artificially separating these things will only hurt you in the long run.

Group 1: The Hurt Purest

These are the people whose life was not working well for them. They have had lots of bad luck and have gone through large amounts of suffering. They came to the spiritual path to end their pain, and it worked. The spiritual path helped them tremendously, and they were able to minimize their pain. Of course this destruction of pain by spiritual process is a good thing. We don't want anyone to suffer, and desiring to end the pain that life sometimes throws at us is a perfectly normal and good motivation to begin with on the spiritual path.

One of the problems with being spiritually motivated because of high amounts of distress is that it opens some people up to the misconception that the world is somehow wrong, evil, or bad. Because the world was hurting this first type of person so much, it makes it easy for them to villainize it and thus be propelled into a binary way of thinking that says that there is a separation between the spiritual and the material.

They may think that, because the world or the material was hurting them, it is all bad and there is nothing good in it. Through spirituality they found considerable peace and happiness, so they may think that the spiritual is the only good. Thus they come up with the idea or subscribe to the myth that the material and the spiritual are entirely different things, material being bad and spiritual being good.

Such people may conclude that to run away from the world, to criticize it, and to minimize any involvement with it, are the best things to do. They think that abstaining from any successful action is better than intelligently pursuing success, financial well-being, or any form of achievement in this world.

> **Contemplation:** Search your mind and heart to see if you have any ill feelings toward the material domain. If so, search to see how much is there because of the suffering you have experienced. This kind of introspections, where we find our limitations, shortcomings, and darker sides, is scary and takes a certain radial honesty. I admire you for attempting it.

1st Pitfall of the Hurt Purist

The Hurt Purist often idealizes a spiritual figure like a Guru, profit, or saint, and projects their misconceived binary idea of a bad material world and a good spiritual world onto that spiritual figure. They imagine that the spiritual figure is "pure" and has no material engagement or involvement, and is therefore perfect. They think that if someone is fully spiritual they cannot be connected to or involved with anything material of this world. It is impossible for them to ever live up to the idea they have created of this person; it is impossible. The Guru or spiritual figure did not abide by these false standards because this idea of so-called purity as a disengagement from the material domain lives in the follower's mind, not the Gurus. The Hurt Purist thus feels inferior; they feel incompetent and just quite useless on the spiritual path. They see that their only hope to fully end their suffering is to become like the mental image they have of the Guru or spiritual figure. But this is impossible, because the idea they have made is a mental fabrication and is unrealistic. Thus the belief system they have built leaves them doomed to feeling like a failure, guilty, and inadequate.

Inherent in all of this is the wrong thinking that the material domain is separate from the spiritual domain.

The fact is, one who is fully enlightened is often a master of dealing with this worldly material domain. We respect such enlightened beings not because they retreat from the world, nor because they may be rich, but because their hearts are full of spiritual love, which is the most beautiful thing in existence.

PERSONAL RESPONSIBILITY

Projecting this false view of spiritual advancement onto someone, even if they are fully enlightened, is detrimental for our spiritual growth and for our sanity in general. This is because such a view is not only based on a fundamental flaw in understanding the nature of life, the world, and the spiritual path, it also encourages people to be lazy. It takes the responsibility off of the individual to practice and progress spiritually, because by projecting one can simply live in a fantasy world, vicariously living out concocted spiritual fetishes through an idealized spiritual figure. Be careful of this. The world is connected, integrated, and part of the spiritual domain. Exactly how this is so will unfold throughout this book.

Simply because there are pain and illusion in the world does not make it bad or wrong. It is not about the world being good or bad; it is about your relationship with it. You can and must one day use this world, which has manifested from the divine, as a tool and offering, in order to enter into the higher blissful spiritual states of Passionate Enlightenment.

A note on detachment: Spiritual advancement comes from Spiritual Surrender and is a passionate, loving relationship with the divine. A detachment from ego-based selfish interest is a natural side effect of spiritual growth. Detachment is an essential, integral, and powerful part of spiritual growth, and for a spiritual figure to truly be highly advanced they must be detached from the vices of the world. But remember there is a stark difference between detachment and disengagement. Spiritual elevation or purity has everything to do with spiritual love, dedication, and detachment, and nothing to do with a disengagement from the elements of this world.

> **Contemplation:** Take a deep and hard look at yourself. Is there a part of you that is avoiding responsibility for either you spiritual growth or even your success and happiness in life? Is there any part of you that sees a Guru's or prophet's purity or spiritual elevation as your saving grace, which thus allows you to take a more passive and lazy role in you spiritual life?
>
> I believe the support and the grace of spiritual guides is essential in spiritual growth. The key distinction here is this: Does my idea of purity make me a passive participant in my spiritual journey, or an active one? As we will learn later, action is part of our Eternal Dharma and is therefore key in our spiritual growth.

2ND PITFALL OF THE HURT PURIST: GUILT

When we are not fully enlightened the majority of what we do is material, because we are still learning to integrate and operate properly with the spiritual. Therefore believing that this material world is separate from the spiritual domain can lead people to feel that they are bad and that something is wrong with them because they spend most of their time interacting with, and thinking of, worldly things. Because of this they may have unhealthy feelings of guilt, which not only sucks the joy and vitality out of life but can even get in the way of their spiritual path. Low self-esteem is not spirituality, and neither is feeling guilty.

Group 2: The Bewildered Materialist

The second group of people are the ones who are doing okay in the world. They may have had some successes, and they are getting a certain degree of pleasure and gratification from life. This group also includes those who may not "have it good" yet, but aspire to it. They want to enjoy and they believe that it is possible to achieve complete happiness through material endeavors alone.

When divorced from the divine, the pleasures of the world have a hypnotic effect and are almost drug like: They dull our minds from being able to see things as they actually are. By indulging, or attempting to indulge, in the pleasures of this world while negating the spiritual, their minds becomes bewildered and they may begin to think that this world is the all in all. They may think that they will do what needs to be done to fulfill their desires and then they will be satisfied. They falsely believe that they have control. This illusion tends to blind them from the suffering of this world and even the suffering caused by their endeavors.

A strong example of this is of a drunkard or drug addict. They think that if they can just get their fix, then they will be happy. But they fail to see that getting their fix and endeavoring in that direction is what is causing their pain. By indulging their vice, they are actually being bound and degraded more, and they are moving further away from happiness, joy, and freedom. The example of a drug addict is a bit of a strong one, but this same principal applies for those of us who are absorbed in this world while neglecting the spiritual domain. This absorption in enjoyment may take the form of one's vices, or other less noticeable mundane actions such as work, family, friends, and so on.

THE SAME PROBLEM

The problem of the "Bewildered Materialist" is the same as the "Hurt Purist" who has come to the spiritual path to run away from the world—creating a separation between the spiritual and the material. Over infatuation with either the spiritual or the material can make us dull to the fact that the material and the spiritual are both just different expressions of the same thing (more details on this in Part 3).

I have seen that some religions propagate the idea of the spiritual/material divide; I think one of the main reasons why they have done and do this is because of the fact that many people who intensely follow and propagate religion are often Hurt Purists.

THE INTEGRATION OF THE SPIRITUAL AND MATERIAL

Even though the spiritual and material are, in a sense, one, they also have their individual natures and functions. They function both separately and in a way that nourishes and supports each other. They are integrated and if we are to be effective and happy in the world we must learn to act in an integrated fashion where both the material and the spiritual are allowed to operate at their fullest and synergize together. This type of integrated action is proper action; it is action in dharma.

For there to be real bliss, power, harmony, and effectiveness, we must appropriately engage and integrate the spiritual and the material into our approach to life. We must learn how to turn every action into a love-based spiritual phenomenon. By doing this, every action becomes a perfect action, every action becomes a spiritual action, every action becomes the most effective action possible, every action leads us to enlightenment, and every action is filled with the greatest cosmic-loving-spiritual-bliss possible for any being to experience in the entirety of all of existence.

GOD SYNDROME

The reason why it can be so hard to properly integrate both the spiritual and the material in our lives is not only because we don't all have the correct information. Enlightenment, though supported by information, is not by any means dependent on it. The real reason we are not constantly swimming in the seductively sweet mellows of pure spiritual bliss is because, more often than not we are afflicted with an ailment I call God Syndrome. I call it this because in essence we ourselves want the position of God.

It is our highest Eternal Dharma to Surrender Spiritually, which means that we are constantly guided by the divine. In order for us to be guided by the divine, the divine must guide. Guiding us and everything in the universe is the dharma of the divine. But because of God Syndrome we don't want to accept that guidance and we want to do the guiding ourselves instead. We want to guide our life, guide others, and guide the whole universe to satisfy our selfish needs. This is not our true dharma, we are not good at it, and therefore when we try to selfishly guide ourselves or others we suffer. Our dharma is to be guided and the dharma of the divine is to guide; God Syndrome is when when we try to switch those roles.

God Syndrome can also be understood as being selfish rather than selfless; the highest happiness is ours when we act selflessly because doing so is our dharma, and selfless action is what brings solace to the soul.

The divine guides everything in the universe according to His/Her or Its desires. This is not selfish, like the ugly selfishness of this world, it is dharmic, meaning that by nature everything in the universe is meant to focus toward the divine and fulfill His/Her desires. So in order to have things function according to dharma, the divine guides all things to focus on itself. God Syndrome is when we try to get everything to focus on us and when we try to make all people and things servants to our desires.

When we focus on loving the divine in perfect spiritual dharma, we are the most satisfied, happy, and content. To fully understand God Syndrome we need to fully understand our own Eternal Dharma, the dharma of the Divine, and the dharma of this world. Then we will be able to clearly understand this often invisible ailment is actually is causing us so much pain and suffering. In essence though, God Syndrome is when we expect that all things should bend to our will and all things are meant for our pleasure. It is when our focus is selfish rather than selfless.

For example, the day my Guru made me a Swami was a superb day for sure. In the Vedic/Indian culture becoming a Swami is a big deal and especially so for someone at the young age of 23 (I was the world's youngest swami.).

There were 10,000 people present at my Sannyasa (Swami) ceremony and it felt like all of them were showering me with love, blessings, affection, and respect. But the problem that day was that when I was meeting people after the ceremony, I was focused on myself. I thought that, because it was such a momentous occasion for me, and I felt like the center of attention, naturally the interactions and conversations were supposed to be about me.

Boy, was I wrong. By focusing on myself, I felt miserable. The best day of my life started to feel horrible. I began to introspect to see what was up. I found that the problem was me being self-centered and focusing on myself rather than the people I was interacting with. I immediately switched and all of sudden I started to become happy again, and the interactions became so much more pleasurable. I had more fun forgetting myself and loving and caring for others on my "big day" than I did talking about myself while people bowed down to me and worshiped me in respect. Being the center and being worshiped offers a brief temporary thrill, and then pretty much becomes miserable. I know this first hand, because in India they worship Swamis. Real happiness lies in dharma, in selfless giving not in selfish action or self-centered focus.

THE MYTH OF DOMINANCE AND CONTROL

There is a destructive myth that is bouncing around society. The myth is that we have control in this world and in life. We falsely think that we can control the results of our actions, when in actuality our ability to control and to dominate is extremely small.

My friends, just think, we are sitting on a lava-filled rock that is floating in the sky. Our planet is a tiny-barely-recognizable spec in our vast galaxy. Our galaxy is only one in an estimated 100 billion galaxies that Hubble has revealed. In fact, the number of 100 billion galaxies is expected to increase to 200 billion as telescope technology improves.

Our miniscule planet is at a perfect distance from the sun to create seasons and create a perfect eco system for life. If that floating, spinning rock upon which we all live, were a few degrees closer to the sun we would be singed, burnt to ashes, and if it were a few degrees away, Earth would be a giant ice cube.

What power do we really have, my friends? What can we really do or control? The not-so-fluffy-for-the-ego truth is: We are insignificant. One of my Gurus used to say that we don't even know how many hairs are on our heads, so what can we really know? We can't even control our simple bodily mechanisms such as digestion and hair growth. The truth is that our knowledge, power, and control is extremely limited. Only delusion or false ego could say otherwise.

Yet the fact is that even though we are so insignificant in the grand scale of existence, we are meant to have power, and enormous amounts of it. The problem is that we often search for the wrong type of power. We wrongly want the power to dominate and control things, to bend them to our selfish desires and whims. We want to be God, but the power that is our birthright, that we are meant to eternally have, is a sweeter power that is accessed through Spiritual Surrender. My friend, do not underestimate this power, for it can and does control God. The divine is eager to taste the love of your heart.

Spiritual growth takes regular practice; go to *www.myspiritualsuccess.com* to get other training from me for free.

PART 2

THE UNPRECEDENTED ELEMENTAL REALITY SYSTEM

CHAPTER 4

INTRODUCING THE UNPRECEDENTED ELEMENTAL REALITY SYSTEM

Congratulations, my friend. I am impressed by your perseverance and determination. This book is an encapsulation of an enormous amount of wisdom, which can be a lot to digest, so good job!

We are now entering Part 2, in which we will explore the nature, or dharma, of the world we live in. By knowing exactly how the world works we get two things:

1. By knowing exactly how the world works, we are more easily able to surrender and trust in the Divine and in the spiritual process of life. All of reality exists and functions for the sole purpose of helping us evolve spiritually. Everything exists only to teach us to connect in passionate spiritual love with the Divine. This can be hard to accept when we don't see and understand how it all works. When we clearly know without a doubt that the purpose, function, and nature of life and the

world are to assist in our spiritual growth, and that the reason for why all things exist is to connect us in spiritual love, it is much easier to trust in life's process and Spiritually Surrender. And as you know, Spiritual Surrender is what will enable us to swiftly glide and passionately grasp loving enlightenment.

2. If you want to be effective in the world you've got to know how things work and how to work them. If you want to have more power and use the world in the most effective way possible, it is crucial to know exactly how it works. The dharma and most powerful and satisfying use of this wisdom comes when we use such newfound power and effectiveness in the service of the Divine. In any case, learning exactly how this world works helps tremendously in, and is vital for, both Effective Action and on the Path to Passionate Enlightenment.

How I Discovered the Unprecedented Elemental Reality System

It was in a small yoga studio in Louisville, Kentucky, and though I was excited and enthused, it dawned on me: I would have to explain it all. These people had come to the event to hear me speak. What had been advertised was that the lecture would be on the power of mantra, a sound vibration or set of words that is supposed to have a mystical or almost magical influence. It is believed that mantras have the ability to affect the physical, emotional, and spiritual domains, and it was my job to show how they actually do that. How was I to explain and justify these subtle and seemingly out-of-world things to a group of people who did not grow up with such experiences? The method is precise and nearly mathematical, yet so often the discussion of such subjects that exist in the non-physical sphere seems like imaginary woo-woo.

In that quaint yoga studio, it was born. At that moment, when all eyes were on me and I had to speak, this "new" way of relating with life and communicating, the ancient 5,000-year-old Vedic wisdom of India, began to blossom.

After the speech, the crowd was happy, but I was also intrigued by this "new" insight on existence. Thoughts on the subject began to percolate in my mind, and everywhere I looked everything seemed different. With this new lens on existence I could never see the world or function in the same way again.

For the next eight years I studied, explored, and expanded this new approach. I drew from my childhood training in the monastery; I drew from the various complex knowledge systems that are part of the Vedas. I consulted with other senior monks, intellectuals, and even scientists. I drew from and cross-referenced this system with the healing arts, such as shiatsu, acupuncture, yoga, reiki, and Jinsin Jitsu. I even used knowledge from martial arts such as Jujitsu and Aiki Jujitsu. What emerged from this all is the Unprecedented Elemental Reality System that you are about to learn.

The fascinating thing is that even though I was researching many different knowledge systems, none of the information conflicted. By nature, all of reality works in harmony, and therefore any true knowledge system will not conflict with any other knowledge system.

This process of discovery has given me so many a-ha moments and brought me so much clarity on the nature of life, reality, and this world, that I must share it. It would be agonizingly selfish if I did not. I can no longer imagine going through life without knowing this.

Originally I intended this book to only be on this Unprecedented Elemental Reality System, but I found that even though the Unprecedented Elemental Reality System is extremely empowering and unique, it is even more powerful and brings even more clarity when it is positioned within the greater context of the spiritual side of the Vedic wisdom and worldview. The Unprecedented Elemental Reality System is not separate from Veda. In fact, it is an explanation and expression of the Vedic wisdom.

The World Is Made of Just 8 Things: The 8 Elements

In essence the Unprecedented Elemental Realty System is a practical study of the eight elements. When examined closely, it becomes apparent that everything in this world, such as all objects, people, and places, are composed of only eight things or elements. These eight elements that make up everything in existence are described in detail in many ancient texts and traditions, my favorite being the wisdom present in the 5,000-year-old Vedic texts of India.

The eight elements are: earth, water, fire, air, ether (sound and space), mind (emotions), intelligence, and false ego/identity. Each of these elements has a dharma, which in this case means a specific way in which the element functions and the natural way in which it interacts with the other elements.

It is important to note that the way that we are approaching the elements here is different than with the periodic table. With the Vedic approach any liquid would be considered water, and any solid would be considered earth. For example, iron and stone are both considered the earth element. In the same way, any light or heat would be fire. The Chinese system of understanding the elements is pretty much the same as the Vedic system, except what we refer to as air is referred to as metal, and ether as wood in the Chinese system.

When you know the nature/dharma of each of these eight elements then you know the world, because everything of the world is made up of only these eight elements. When you know how to direct these elements you have power. When you act from your dharma and use the elements according to their dharma you have Universal Alignment, which means the entire universe acts to support and enhance what you are doing.

Practice: Act in Universal Alignment

Before doing anything important, such as writing a paper, going on a date, organizing a meeting, closing a business deal, cooking dinner, shopping, and so forth, do the following:

1. Stop to take at least three deep breaths and relax. This brings your body and mind into connection and allows you to think clearly.
2. Remind yourself what your Beneficial Temporary Dharma is (see page 44 in Chapter 2), then ask yourself if the action you are about to perform is an execution of, or in alignment with, your Beneficial Temporary Dharma.

3. Remember that your Eternal Dharma is to serve the Divine in love and devotion. Ask yourself if the action you are about to perform is an execution of, or in alignment with your Eternal Dharma, meaning, it be an offering of love or pleasing to the Divine in some way.

4. Think of the dharma of the tools, objects, people, or things that will be involved in the task.

5. Try your best to use every component of the project according to its dharma.

The more dharma in the whole endeavor, the more the project is in Universal Alignment. The more Universal Alignment, the more successful, fulfilling, and effective the project will be.

If the action is in alignment with your Eternal Dharma, meaning it is done for the pleasure of the divine, then the action becomes a spiritual practice and aids in the process of advancing to Passionate Enlightenment. This is Full Universal Alignment.

The 5 Physical Elements

The elements are best viewed in what I call the "Elemental Spectrum": They go from subtle to physical or physical to subtle, and this order has profound significance. I always look to this spectrum when I am trying to understand something or solve a problem. We will go into each element and the significance of this order in more detail later, but here is an extremely quick overview of the eight elements. Go to eternaldharmabook.com to download the Elemental Spectrum. It will help you understand this system with ease.

Earth

Like all the elements, earth exists in many forms. Of course it is the ground and soil, but more importantly for us seeking to be effective, earth is tangible measurable results, practicality, grounded-ness, steadiness, rhythm, and structure. All things that are solid both physically and metaphorically are the earth element. (Quick tip: Use the element of earth to create tangible results.)

Water

All that is liquid is water, as are the qualities of flow, adaptability, sensitivity, and nourishment. (Quick tip: Use the principle of water to enhance relationships.)

Fire

Flames, heat, light, electricity, action, power, clarity, vision, vigor, and drive are all different expressions of the fire element. (Quick tip: Use the qualities of fire in leading.)

Air

Oxygen and wind are the air element, but more importantly the subtle energy known as *Prana* in Sanskrit and *Chi* in Chinese is the air element. In the Unprecedented Elemental Reality System, we often see air in its form of raw unused power or potential. (Quick tip: Use air to increase physical energy.)

Ether/Space

The space in which all things exist and vibrations, especially sound vibrations, are the ether element. (Quick tip: Bring ether into harmony to bring balance and harmony to the rest of the elements.)

The 3 Subtle Elements

These elements are "non-matter." They are not physically tangible and are very hard to measure, yet, as you will learn, they are the most important and powerful, and undeniably real.

Mind

In this system the mind is defined as both your emotions and the constant internal dialogue that goes on inside your head. (Quick tip: Control your mind to be peaceful and focused.)

Intelligence

Intelligence is information, data, and thought. It is also the ability to "crunch" this data and calculate what the smartest course of action is. (Quick tip: Know before you go. In life we often act before acquiring enough information and calculating what the best course of action is. It is always best to act in knowledge.)

Ego/Identity

This is your self-concept; your paradigms, beliefs, and world view. It is also the understanding and view of what something is. (Quick tip: Align your ego/identity with your desires to eliminate internal turmoil and thus become more effective.)

Many Ancient Arts and Sciences Are Based on the 8 (or 5) Elements

Many ancient cultures, traditions, and sciences deal with or are based in the concept of the elements. Acupuncture, Chinese and Ayurvedic medicine, kung fu, Shamanism, swordsmanship, yoga, and so many other arts are deeply rooted in the philosophy of the elements. I find this fascinating because it means that people repeatedly and successfully use and used the knowledge of the elements in very high-stake situations.

Sword Dual to the Death

In a sword duel to the death, you really can't afford any imagined or theoretical woo-woo myths: What you know and do must be real, or you die. The knowledge of the elements that you are about to learn is as real as the breath you breathe and the ground you stand on. The legendary swords-man Miyamoto Musashi of Japan, who is considered one of the greatest fighters in history, dedicated the last years of his life to writing *The Book of Five Rings*, an explanation of how to use the knowledge of the elements to win sword fights. He used this wisdom to win myriad duals to the death against Japan's best Samurai.

Acupuncture

Every day, acupuncturists across the globe use the knowledge of the ele-ments to cure patients of agonizing ailments. I personally witnessed a high fever decrease in only 15 minutes using the technique of five-element acupuncture. I also have a close friend who is an acupuncturist in Hawaii who has saved several people from dying of heart attacks with this same system. I regularly use acupuncture to cure stomach aches, headaches, and colds.

In my view, if thousands of people for thousands of years have success-fully and consistently won wars, battles, and fights, and people have con-sistently saved lives and cured "incurable" diseases with the knowledge of the elements, then it is not only plausible that this knowledge is real, but that it could exponentially help me in my life to do and create the things I want.

Spiritual Paths

On the spiritual side, Vedic literature teaches about the five or eight ele-ments and their involvement on the spiritual path. Though I am not an expert in Taoism or Zen, I believe that these systems are also rooted in an understanding of the elements. As you learn more and grow you will find the many ways in which knowledge of the elements is a strong building block to construct your spiritual temple of love for the Divine.

Where Are the Elements?

When one hears that the elements make up everything in all of existence, they may start to think, "What does this all mean?" Really, where are the elements anyway? It can be hard to grasp the concept of "everything in all of existence" but when I say it, I almost literally mean it: Every single thing that exists in this world and beyond, with the exception of spiritual things like the soul and God, is a mixture of the eight elements.

The computer that I'm using to write this book is made up of the elements, the chair that I'm sitting on is made up of the elements, this house and all of the objects in it are made up of the elements. Every tree, animal, and plant in the forest, as well as every item sold in Walmart—all are made of the elements.

The galaxies are made of the elements. Our bodies are also made up of the elements. The medical sciences that understand the elements such as acupuncture and Ayurveda, say that there is fire in the digestive system, that our blood and other bodily fluids are the water element, and that the air element lives in the lungs and large intestines. They say that disease is caused when the elements are out of balance in the body.

The elements even exist in different psychologies and mindsets. In combat, the classic way of using the knowledge of the elements is to predict your opponent's next move by ascertaining which element dominates the psychology and consciousness of your opponent. In a fight or battle, you can even choose which element to imbibe in order to defeat your opponent. For example, water tames fire, so if your enemy is fiery, and thus attacks with lots of motivation, passion, and flare, you can choose to be water-like and defeat him or her by being adaptive, fluid, and flowing like water.

The elements also exist in the emotions. The ancient Vedic health systems of yoga and Ayurveda say that there are different energy channels in the body and that each of these channels is represented by particular elements. They also say that there are energy centers in the body that are known as chakras. Each chakra represents, imbibes, and vibrates the energy of a different element, and our emotions and tendencies are very much affected by how strong each chakra vibrates. From this we can see that when we refer to the elements, we do not only refer to the physical tangible element substances, such as actual earth, water, fire, and so forth, but also to the qualities of these elements, which can exist in intangible ways such as in different mindsets, chakras, or energies. All of existence is made up of the eight elements in either their physical state or their vibrational energy.

> **Contemplation:** Rub your hands together until they become hot. Heat (fire) exists in your hands. Now clap your hands. Either (sound) exists in your hands. Now slice your hands. Water (blood) exists in your hands. Just kidding! Please don't cut yourself. But do notice how the elements are everywhere.

5 vs. 8 Elements: Some Elements Are Subtle and Some Are Physical

If you are familiar with the elements, then you may have heard that some sciences deal with four elements, whereas other sciences deal with five. It may therefore take you by surprise to know that there are eight elements.

This observation actually opens a very crucial and deep understanding of how the elements work. Not all elements are created equal. Some elements are subtle; other elements are physical. The more physical an element, the easier it is to measure, to touch, to see, to smell, and to have physical contact with. The more subtle the element is, the more volatile, flowing, intangible, and harder to perceive.

For example, take air. Air is a very subtle element, yet it is undoubtedly real. If it did not exist we would all suffocate, yet we cannot see it with the naked eye. Air is invisible and intangible to certain senses. On the other hand, earth is a very tangible and measurable element. It is the most physical of all the elements: Anyone can see, touch, smell, and taste. The existence of earth is undebatable and undeniable, whereas the existence of air is debatable to the naked eye.

In the same way, some elements are even more subtle than air. They are harder to see, harder to touch, and harder to perceive, yet their existence is also undeniable. They are: ether (space/sound), mind, intelligence, and false ego. Many sciences only deal with the first four or five physical elements, as these elements are more physical, more tangible, and thus easier to understand and perceive. Sciences that are focused on one specific area, such as medical or architectural sciences, approach their craft through only the first four or five physical elements. Yet a complete science, intended to illuminate every facets of life, like the one presented in this book, must also include the other three more subtle elements to be fully accurate and impactful.

Those who speak about four elements refer to earth, water, fire, and air. Those who speak about five elements include those four, plus ether (also understood as sound and space; how both sound and space are the same thing will make sense when you get to Chapter 8). Those who refer to the eight elements speak about those five elements, with the addition of mind, intelligence, and false ego.

CHAPTER 5

ELEMENTAL FOUNDATIONS

Each element has a different dharma, or a unique nature and a different set of qualities. Though each element in a sense stands on its own and has its own dharma, it is not independent: Its existence is very much connected to, dependent on, and influenced by the other elements. By understanding how the elements are connected, it is easier to understand the elements themselves. This is why when training people to harness the power of the elements, I often start with teaching the connection of the elements. This part of the Unprecedented Elemental Reality System will empower you the most.

The key to knowing the connection among the elements is simple: Just visualize the elements in a line, sequenced from subtle to physical, or from physical to subtle. This order is extremely significant because the physical is a condensation of the subtle, and the subtle creates the physical. Many people are already aware of this. They know that subtle things, like their mindset, create their life, and that thoughts, education, and feelings affect final outcomes. Great philosophies, theories, and books have been created from observing this phenomenon. In recent times, teachers of the law of attraction have become a dime a dozen, but unfortunately

I have yet to find a mainstream teacher (granted I have not studied all courses) that can clearly and specifically explain exactly how and why the subtle creates the physical. Much of the knowledge on the subject floats in the realm of inexplicable woo-woo-ness, and for me that just doesn't cut it. Luckily I was graced to stumble upon this Unprecedented Elemental Reality System that brings clear and credible insight to exactly how the subtle creates the physical and exactly how the subtle is more powerful. What a relief. By visualizing the elements in a progression from subtle to physical, you begin to see how creation takes place.

If you are creating anything, be it an art project, business, building, or relationship, you can see exactly which point in the process you may need to adjust to get the results you want. But there is so much more to this system than just creating. The physical supports and tames the subtle, and the subtle, being of a superior quality and more powerful than the physical, magnifies the physical. My friend, this is such a large subject that the next chapters are devoted to it.

There are many reasons for seeing the elements as a continuum progressing from subtle to physical, beyond what is outlined here. Your first task in learning the Unprecedented Elemental Reality System is to get familiar with the order of the elements from physical to subtle, or subtle to physical.

Memorization

In the modern era of inexhaustible amounts of ever-increasing information, I have found that there is little emphasis put on memorization. Perhaps this is because information is easily available on the internet so we can just search for whatever we need to know. Or perhaps it is easier to be a passive consumer of information than an active learner. In any case, memorization of certain key things allows us to have a wealth of the information ready to use when we need it. Not all things need to be memorized—I personally use a plethora of checklists in my life—but there are few key things that are best stored in our head, and I suggest that the order of the elements is one of them.

Legend has it that the Vedas were originally taught by memorization. The Guru would speak an entire scripture, which more often than not was composed in elegant Sanskrit poetry, and the disciple would memorize the whole thing by only hearing it. Legend says that this was the normal and standard way of learning Veda. As time progressed and human intelligence devolved, the Gurus decided to write the Vedic wisdom down, which took place about 5,000 to 7,000 years ago. I often refer to the Vedic knowledge as "5,000-year-old wisdom" because 5,000 to 7,000 years is what is documented and accepted as fact, but the truth is that if we look at what is actually written in the Vedas, we can see that the wisdom therein is far older.

When we were young in the monastery, every morning we were taught about three Sanskrit verses from the Vedas. We had no book; the teacher would teach by reciting the verse, we would repeat it back, and after a considerable number of repetitions we would have memorized the verse. Later, when traveling with my Guru around the world, he would have me memorize a verse on my own each day. I would report to him in the evening to recite the verse. Having quite a lot of experience with it, I have found that memorization is a like a muscle: The more you do it, the better at it you become, and everybody has a different amount of strength.

How to Memorize Anything

Here is a great system for memorization. It is designed specifically for memorizing Vedic verses, but it will work for anything. (I find it interesting to note that I discovered the entire Unprecedented Elemental Reality System by contemplating only one verse that I had memorized, from one of the best Vedic scriptures: the Bhagavad Gita [Chapter 7, verse 4].)

1. Repeat a small fragment of what you are memorizing out loud 33 times. (33 is a good number, but it may need to be more or less depending on how strong your memory muscle is. I know some people for whom only two or three times is enough.) For example: Memorizing the order of the elements: earth, water, fire,

air, ether, mind, intelligence, and false ego. Pick a small fragment, a bite-sized chunk such as "earth, water, fire," and repeat it 33 times out loud.

2. Repeat the same chunk "earth, water, fire" 33 times, under your breath, whispering.

3. Now repeat the same chunk in your mind, with no sound and without your lips moving 33 times.

4. Repeat the same process (33 times out loud, 33 times under your breath, 33 times in your mind), for the next two chunks: "air, ether" and "mind, intelligence, and false ego."

5. Put the first two chunks together and do the same 33, 33, 33 method with them united: "earth, water, fire, air, ether."

6. Repeat the process with all three chunks together: "earth, water, fire, air, ether, mind, intelligence, and false ego."

By now you should have the elements or whatever you are memorizing permanently imprinted in your brain, ready to access whenever you need.

You may need to refresh your memory of some things after some time, as memorization does fade in time.

The Subtle Is More Important and Powerful Than the Physical

My friends, here is one of my favorite and most insightful parts of this Unprecedented Elemental Reality System. Because we have already learned that some elements are subtle and some are physical, I am happy to say that the subtle ones—the ones that are the hardest to see, touch, and perceive—are actually the most powerful and the most important ones. If you always remember that the subtle is more powerful and important than the physical, you will always be able to access a superior energy for greater power and effectiveness. This is a fundamentally important point that we must train our minds to always see if we are to be powerful.

You cannot have any power or success if you don't harness the power of these subtle elements and the subtle realm. Anyone who has ever had any significant power and influence has been a master at dealing with the subtle domain. I am not talking about magic, witchcraft, voodoo, or anything of the sort; I am speaking about the power of emotions, perceptions, numbers, ideas, time, beauty, love, information, education, and all the other wonderful things that you cannot touch physically or lock in a box.

Losing Your Power

People have lost their power because they have been focusing on and valuing the wrong things. Their attention has been on the wrong end of the elemental spectrum. It has been on physical, touchable things rather than in the realm of the subtle. People have been focusing on things such as their bodies, cars, houses, computers, food, and toys rather than the subtle, more powerful elements such as their mind and identity—which is what creates those fun physical things.

What You Really Want Is Subtle

Ironically, if you look closely, people only want physical things, like cars and handbags, for the subtle things that it will provide them. A new car or handbag is desirable because it makes you look good, which feels good and gets you some kind of approval, love, or admiration from people. So really you don't want the handbag: You want approval, love, admiration, self-esteem, and good feelings, which are all subtle. The subtle, again, is more important than the physical.

> **Contemplation:** Make a list of two or three things you want. Then list the subtle benefit, the thing you really want. Here's an example:
> What I say I want: a better house
> What I really want: to feel more comfortable and safe

Subtle Power and Passionate Enlightenment

You may wonder: What does this all have to do with Passionate Enlightenment? I will give you another hint, different from what we already covered about the importance of integrating the spiritual and the material: Passionate Enlightenment is the most subtle thing in existence. Therefore, it is the most powerful and most important aspect of all reality. Once you realize and clearly see the sheer power and value of the subtle realm, you will look for the most subtle thing, which is Passionate Enlightenment. If I am completely open with you, I am much more excited for you to learn Passionate Enlightenment over anything else, because that is what will nourish your spirit the most and cause the greatest lasting benefit possible: To love in Passionate Enlightenment is your Eternal Dharma—and it is my dharma to help you and others as much as humanly possible to taste this rare and exciting spiritual bliss.

Another thing to note is that, because the subtle creates the physical, attaining Passionate Enlightenment gives you the superpower to be able to create whatever you want. It is defined by selfless love, though, so once you get it, you will probably not use it in the same ways that you may be imagining now.

Unbendable Arm Technique

When I was studying jujitsu we learned a technique that immediately lets you experience how the subtle is more powerful than the physical by making your arm unbendable only using your mind.

Part 1:

1. Get a partner.
2. Both partners should be standing.
3. Have the weaker one (partner A) clench a fist and put his or her wrist on the shoulder of the stronger partner (partner B). Make sure the elbow is pointing down (or almost down, so you do not hurt yourself).
4. Partner A: Put two hands on the inside of the elbow between the bicep and forearm of partner B.

5. When both partners agree, have Partner B extend his or her arm: B, use all your physical strength and muscles to not let Partner A bend it. At the same time, partner A should strongly push down and try to bend the arm. As soon as the arm bends, stop. (Generally what happens is the arm bends without much difficulty, if both partners are of equal strength, because partner A is using two arms while partner B is only using one.)

This first part of the exercise is just to establish what would happen normally if power was just physical.

Part 2:

1. Partner B: This time open your fingers, point them out straight, and keep them together. Make sure your thumb is pointing upward.

2. Breathe in deeply three times and relax after each breath, and become present in your body.

3. Look over the shoulder behind partner A and imagine that there is a huge raging fire behind him or her that is insatiable. It cannot be stopped, and the flames are roaring.

4. Imagine that your arm is a thick, highly powerful water hose that is shooting water into the raging fire.

5. See that as the pressure increases on your arm, the pressure of the water increases and more water shoots out of your arm and into this fire.

6. Keep your eyes and mind focused on this visualization.

7. Partner A: at this time begin to put pressure on the arm. Start slowly so that partner B can keep focused on the visualization. Increase the pressure until you are pushing as hard as you can.

8. Stop either when partner B has pushed as hard as possible or if the arm bends. The whole exercise only needs to take a few seconds. It does not need to be long.

If done properly, the arm will be impossible or much harder to bend. Partner B may not be able to notice it because it takes less energy than when using only muscle, but partner A should feel how much harder or how impossible it is to bend the arm when the meditation is done. What generally happens is the arm bends when partner B loses focus.

The reason why this works is because—you guessed it—the subtle is more powerful than the physical. Though all the elements have been engaged in this exercise, a simplified explanation of what was going on is that through the visualization, the intelligence element guides the chi or prana (powerful subtle energies that belong to the air element) through the arm. This subtle energy is more power than physical muscles, so as long as the energy is moving strongly through the arm it is impossible to bend with brute strength.

The whole point of this is to give you firsthand experience of how the subtle is more powerful than the physical.

Warning: Do not do this technique if you have any injuries or if you feel that it may harm you in any way. You are solely responsible for making sure you do not get hurt with this. To watch a fun video go to your bonuses at *eternaldharmabook.com/bonus*

Money, Relationships, and Getting a Feel for the Unprecedented Elemental Reality System

This point of the subtle being more important and powerful than the physical is so important that I'll illustrate it clearly and show you exactly how the subtle is the most important and most powerful force in the world. To do this we will look at how this principle and system works in both money and relationships. These examples should also give you a preliminary feel of how to use the Unprecedented Elemental Reality System.

Money

What is money? I have asked this question and researched it for several years, and the subject is not simple. The fact is, though we see money as something solid and tangible, it is actually not. A dollar bill is simply a piece of paper that we all agree is worth something; it is only valuable because we agree it is. If we changed that agreement and chose to see it as less or more valuable, then its value would change; there is little to no intrinsic value in it.

But yet money is so valuable that the whole world runs on it. Our collective agreement is what gives that piece of paper value. Surprisingly, we as citizens of the world are always changing our agreement on the value of a dollar; if you look at any forex chart this becomes obvious. The same dollar bill in my pocket goes up and down in value every minute because the subtle forces of the emotions, perceptions, and agreements of the masses are always changing.

Entire nations and economies depend on the confidence people have in the currency. If the public loses confidence in the currency, the currency becomes useless; when that happens people starve, topple their governments, riot, and start wars.

Think about that: Collective confidence in a piece of paper is not physical. You cannot touch it or hold it; it only exists intangibly in the minds and emotions of people, yet it is so powerful that it can cause wars, starvation, and chaos. This is what I mean when I say that the subtle is more powerful and important than the physical.

The entire economy runs on emotions, which are not physical. If people feel happy and safe, they spend, and the economy grows. If they are scared, on the other hand, they stop spending and a nation or the world goes into a recession. Emotions are subtle.

Many sources, among them MarketWatch.com (*www.marketwatch .com/story/this-is-how-much-money-exists-in-the-entire-world-in-one -chart-2015-12-18*), point to the fact that 85 to 95 percent of money in the world is not even printed; it is digital and exists as a number on a bank's computer screen. Yet, those little numbers are so powerful. Digital numbers on a screen are information: They are subtle, not physical.

I used to think that money was backed by gold, oil, or some sort of commodity, but modern-day currency is not. And even if it was, the principle of the subtle being more important than the physical would still hold, because the value or price of gold or any other commodity depends on supply and demand. The principle of supply and demand is just that: a principle. It is subtle, not physical.

I want to clearly show you how the subtle, which is sometimes referred to as non-matter, is more important than matter, or the physical. Knowing this is key to not only understanding the Unprecedented

Elemental Reality System but also comprehending life and the way that the Universe works; this is key in being more effective.

> **Quick Tip: Making More Money**
>
> If you want to make more money, look at and tweak the three most subtle elements: mind, intelligence, and false ego.
>
> **Ego/Identity:** This is your identity; the beliefs you have about yourself; how you see yourself. If you see yourself as poor, then you will always be poor, because you will act, think, and feel as a poor person does. If you somehow get lots of money, you will spend it incorrectly, invest it wrongly, and lose it. If you identify as a rich person, even if you start out broke, you will find a way to generate what you see as your rightful wealth, because that is who you are and the kind of person you see yourself as.
>
> **Intelligence:** This is information. The more you learn about finances, business, and the nature of money, the better equipped you will be to manage and create it. Education is key in wealth creation, so learn as much as you can about investing, accounting, business, and so forth, and you will be able to make and keep much more money.
>
> **Mind:** In the context of the elements, the mind element is the emotions. To generate better finances, examine what your feelings are about money. If you have negative feelings toward it, you will have less of it, because you won't want to manage it, learn more about it, or deal with it. Increase the feelings of happiness and joy around money, and you will be more able deal with it and thus be able to make more of it.

Relationships

Relationships are of utmost importance to our life, yet how much of a relationship is actually physical? Even the most sensual of relationships has a limited amount of physical sex, cuddles, and touching. The majority of what defines a relationship is in the subtle domain. Feelings are subtle, communication is subtle, and we should never underestimate what story and ego play in a relationship.

When reading romance novels what enthralls us the most is the story of how the two lovers came together, what the tragedy is that's holding them apart, and so on. These stories exist in minds and words, two things that are subtle. If you think back to your most treasured romantic memories, what makes them special is the subtle not the physical. Yes, the physical was important, but it was the feelings you had, the thrill of a new unique situation, and the passion that made it special. The value of the physical was contingent on the love and excitement of the moment. You could have the same physicality without the feelings and story, and the memory would not be one of your most cherished.

What is a relationship? It is a connection, an agreement, a set of feelings, a shared history, an exchange of words, or a social contract. All of these things are non-matter; they are subtle.

Tip: Who Am I in This Relationship?

Because relationships of all kinds, such as with family, friends, lovers, business partners, social groups, and God, are fundamentally important in our happiness and success, this tip will jump straight to the most subtle and most powerful element of them all: false ego or identity.

If a relationship is strained, or you want to increase the strength of it, you need to increase the identity in the relationship. This means that you want to clearly identify with the relationship.

For example, my siblings and I never really lived together. We have a large age gap, and I went to live in a monastery when I was 11. So the truth is that I have spent a lot more time, have a lot more in common, and have more history with several of my friends, yet my relationship with my siblings is stronger and deeper. Why is this? It is because of the element of false ego/identity. My siblings and I identify and believe we have a bond that is unbreakable. No matter what happens we will always be siblings; it is something that cannot change; we choose to believe that you cannot divorce you sister or brother. Because we have this identity, our relation-ships are strong and deep.

On the other hand, I know of some people who have different identity with regard to a sibling. They may have even grown up with them but decided, for whatever reason, that even though this other person was born from the same parents has little significance. Thus they don't identify with the relationship much and the bond is not so strong. Identity is a choice.

(The subject of love relationships and connection is a large subject, and I shall cover this fully in another book.)

Tip 1: Relationship is driven by identity and identity is affected most by the elements before and after it, which are desire (not technically an element, more on this later) and intelligence. Remember to refer to the Elemental Spectrum Image available with your bonus: *eternaldharmabook.com/bonus*

1. Desire (most subtle and most powerful).

    Part 1: Write down who you want this person to be to you. Do you want them to be your best friend, husband, wife, business partner, etc.?

    Part 2: Write down at least seven reasons why you want this relationship with them. Of course, the more reasons you write, the better. Example: I want so and so to be my busi-ness partner because (1) we have the same mission, (2) she is intelligent, etc.

2. Identity/false ego.

    Get clear on where the relationship really is. Clearly write down who they are to you, and who you are to them. Example: I see this person as my teacher. This person sees me as a friend.

3. Intelligence.

    Use the element of intelligence to figure out and write down what you need to do so that you both have the same iden-tity in the relationship. This will take some creative thinking. I suggest you do a brainstorming session in which you write down all your different ideas, and then choose the strongest ideas to follow through with. Example: 1. Stop seeing him as my teacher and see him as a friend because that's how he sees me, and friendship is a better foundation for creating a business partnership. 2. Invite him for a friendly activity to deepen the relationship. 3. Propose a business partnership.

Tip 2: If a relationship is stressed, solidify the identity of the relationship. This is how:

1. Make sure the identity of the relationship is established. If it is not, do the exercise in Tip 1.
2. Remind yourself of the identity of the relationship. Doing this in writing is more solidifying.
3. Remind your partner of the identity of the relationship. Be sure to do this with love and empathy.
4. Use all of the elements to strengthen the relationship, which simply means to do, say, think, feel, and give things that will strengthen the relationship identity.

Take this example: The relationship of husband and wife is stressed.

1. The couple is married, so the relationship is established. (If the stress is so much that they may be reconsidering the identity of the relationship, or it has already changed, complete the process outlined in Tip 1.)
2. Declare to yourself that I am _____'s wife/husband. Think about the wedding, the honeymoon, the proposal, and all the things that make you husband and wife.
3. Watch your wedding video with your partner, revisit the place where you had your first date, listen to "your song."
4. Buy each other gifts, reminisce with your partner about happy experiences together and tell those stories to others, hug, cook, go out for dinner, and so forth. (The possibilities are endless.) Note: None of this will work if the other person does not have sufficient desire. We are not manipulating here.

Focus on the Subtle

Focus your attention on the subtle. It is the most powerful, valuable, and important aspect of creation/existence. The more you focus there, the better off you are. The most subtle thing in existence is the Spiritual Domain.

CHAPTER 6

EARTH'S STEADINESS, WATER'S FLAVOR, AND FIRE'S PASSION

I will start by describing the physical elements and progress to the more subtle ones because the physical elements are easier to understand. Yet you will discover that the subtle elements are not only the more powerful and important, but they are also the least understood.

This book is a training manual. I want you to be able to refer back to it whenever you have questions, problems, or needs in the future. Therefore I have laid out the next section as a reference guide so that when you are in a pickle you can come back (you don't need to spend your time memorizing this; just the order of the elements is enough) and easily find the specific details you need to accomplish your objective.

I am giving you an information toolbox. There are many ways you can use a hammer. Once you have that hammer and have seen it being used in one or two ways, you can figure out new ways to use it to serve your purposes. Similarly, I am giving you information about the elements along with a few examples and tips of how you can use this information, but there are millions of ways you can use it, and for the best results you will need to apply this information in a multitude of ways, beyond the examples outlined here in this book.

Earth

Earth is the most physical, tangible, compact, dense, and solid of all elements. It is the condensation of all the other elements and imbued with their energy. All things rest upon the Earth, for it is the solid, steady bedrock that supports everything and everyone.

The existence of earth is undeniable. People may doubt or question the other more subtle elements, such as mind or false ego, but nobody argues the existence of physical, tangible things such as earth.

Qualities: Solid, hard, grounded, concrete, cold or cooling, stable, steady, mature, easily measurable, structured, straightforward, fixed, accepting, condensed, slow, reliable, disciplined, earthy, practical, cautious, reliable, conservative, realistic, rhythmic.

Negative Qualities: Lethargic, slow, dull, passive, boring.

Dharma: Earth strives to make things steady, to ground, to bring peace and clarity, and to cool things down, and loves measurable predictability. Earth does not like variables, and wants everything simple and steady. With earth, everything fits into clearly defined boxes such as spreadsheets and schedules, and all rules that are set in stone.

Visual: The simple, blunt, heavy-set construction worker.

Quantity in Existence: Surprisingly, even though we live on planet Earth there is less earth on the planet than any other element. Because earth is a condensation of all the other elements, it only makes sense that there is less volume of earth. It takes a large amount of coal to make a smaller amount of diamonds: Diamonds are compressed coal. In the same way, earth is a compact compression of all the other elements. It is the most dense, and thus there is a smaller amount of it and it takes up less space.

From this we can see that those things with earth-like qualities such as clarity, tangible results, and concrete communication are rare in the world. Many people can talk but only few can do, so if you find a partner or employee that imbibes the qualities of earth like clear communication and has created tangible results, take care of them. They are hard to come by and they can and will produce solid and grounded results in the future. Earth doesn't like change so you can rely on them.

What to Use Earth For: Increase the earth element when you want clarity, stability, predictability, and something long term that will stand the test of time. Earth is for tangible results; think buildings, cash, statistics, muscle, objects—anything measureable. If something is fickle, unreliable, or confusing and you don't want it to be so, increase the earth element.

You increased the earth element by choosing to imbibe the qualities of earth. This means being concrete in your communication, actions, and thoughts. This can be done by clearly defining what you are communicating, and writing things down rather than just speaking them. Earth is measureable and is all about measuring things with numbers, facts, and figures. When you compartmentalize ideas into anything that is measurable, such as a diagram or spreadsheet, you are acting in the earth energy and will reap the fruits of what the earth element has to offer.

Activities such as record-keeping, accounting, physical labor, building, and anything with discipline, clarity, simplicity, and focus all exist in the earth element's domain.

Examples

EFFECTIVE IN BUSINESS

The very nature and purpose of business is permeated by the qualities of earth. Business, like earth, is about stability, sustainability, practicality, and tangible results. To bring stability and sustainability to a business, infuse it with more earth-like qualities.

To do this, create systems, processes, and rules within the company that are "set in stone"—that are immovable like mountains. Earth is about measurability, so put systems in place that measure every aspect of the business. This is not limited to accounting and time management. Measure everything possible, even things such as time spent with customers, air quality, and how many times employees and customers smile. Whatever is not measured and systemized is lacking in earth like qualities and therefore will not be steady or produce reliable results. There will be a constant crisis in areas lacking earthiness and crisis is something you want to avoid in business.

Be simple like earth: Create simple systems and measure results. If the results are not what you want, you need to build a system that will create the results you want.

A Dharma Business

To find the best new system, you need to adopt the adaptability and sensitivity of water, because it is water that comes before earth in the spectrum of the elements. In truth, all the elements need to be present in proper balance for an ultra-effective business, which I call a "dharma business." A dharma business is in alignment and harmony with the very nature of this world and life, and thus harnesses the power of the universe. This means that by being in dharma, all nature, elements, planets, and even God help and serve to bring your business to success.

Dharma businesses serve the world the best; make the happiest employees, entrepreneurs, and customers; are spiritually enlightening; and make the most money.

IN RELATIONSHIPS

Relationships are complex; they are full of emotion, flavor, and change. This is part of what keeps them entertaining and interesting, yet we also still seek security, stability, and tranquility in our relationships. In order for home to be homey, we need to feel safe and supported in our relationships at home. Therefore the earth element is a must for balancing relationships that are too fiery (fire) or too emotional (water) and unsustainable. If you have such a relationship or just want and need more grounded stability in a relationship, be earthlike, which means be clear and concrete in your communication. Create clear boundaries, make clear agreements, and do all of this with the unchange-ability of the Himalayas. Doing so will make it easy to see exactly where the relationship stands and will create a strong foundation from which to build a peaceful, balanced, and drama-free (or drama-minimal) relationship.

In Health

Routine is the earth element. Routine is the cornerstone of health. Followers of the ancient health science of Ayurveda are very strict with their habits; they make sure that they wake up and go to sleep at the same times every day and they eat at the same times. This puts the body in a rhythm and thus the body can prepare to perform the appropriate functions optimally.

The Western approach also recognizes the importance of rhythm, specifically in reference to our sleep cycle, or circadian rhythm. When we wake up and get exposed to light, our body produces serotonin to give us energy; and when night comes our body produces melatonin to make us drowsy and put us to sleep. We have an internal clock and by being regular with it we avoid many sicknesses.

If we take this concept one step further we see that the world and the universe also has a rhythm: The sun rises and sets with mathematical precision, the moon has a cycle, and the seasons come and go every year. If we align our daily routine with the natural flow of nature, then these forces become supportive for our health. If we do not, our health is harmed.

Earth Tips

There are so many ways to align your "earth-like" routine with the flow of nature, but here are some tips: Eat your largest meal when the sun is at its highest point, at noon. Eat most of your heavy meals while it is still light. Sleep when it's dark, and do calm, restful, and passive activities when the sun is down, thus harnessing the tranquility of the moon. Do strenuous work during the day, harnessing the power of the sun. Eat seasonal fruits and vegetables.

Earth Activities

Things you can do to increase the earth element include studying, accounting, making lists, using spreadsheets, and using productivity apps that schedule and measure your progress. I use a Pomodoro app and find it quite useful for increasing earth-like action.

You see, earth is all about taking more subtle intangible things and making them tangible and measurable. It is the condensation of all the other elements. So anything that takes an intangible—such as focus, time, style, and ideas—and provides a visible structure to them is earth-like.

Extras for Earth

I suggest not trying to doctor yourself from this book. Health systems based on the elements, such as five-element acupuncture and Ayurveda, take several years of university study to practice. Nor do I suggest any yogic or astrological practice solely based on this book. I mention these extras and how they are associated with the elements for two reasons:

1. So you can see the divine harmony and interconnectedness of all things in the universe and admire the Divine for making such a fabulously complex and perfectly harmonious universe. He/She likes that.
2. So you can better understand how this all works and make meaningful tweaks and adjustments in your life as your knowledge grows.

The Vedic knowledge is vast and covers many areas.

In Medicine: Stomach and spleen.

Chakra: 1st, Muladhara known as the Base/Root.

Astrology: Saturn, Jupiter, Mars and Taurus, Virgo, Capricorn.

Sense and Sense Object: Each of the five physical elements is connected to a particular sense and sense object. (We will not get into this much, but this is good information for when you start to get creative and apply this knowledge in ways that are not explicitly outlined.)

Knowledge Acquiring Sense: Nose.

The Ekadashi Fast

Ekadashi is a Vedic spiritual practice that has many wonderful healthy side effects. This superb practice is performed by fasting two times a month in rhythm with the moon. It is the 11th lunar day in a fortnight. The gravitational pull of the moon affects bodies of water on this planet. This is most visibly seen with the changing tides of the ocean. This pull also affects the water in our bodies. Therefore two days a month the water in our body is disturbed and uneasy. If we eat heavy foods at this time it is hard for our body to assimilate them, and the food weakens our body rather than nourishing it. Therefore on these two Ekadashi days people fast.

A full fast from both food and water is best, but generally eating only fruits and vegetables and avoiding beans and grains is enough. Definitely don't eat any meat on these days. By fasting and eating lightly the body and digestive system gets a chance to rest and heal.

Ekadashi days also have a spiritual significance. Meditation and mantra chanting are enhanced during this time, so lots of mantra meditation is highly recommended.

In the monastery we would sometimes not even sleep and would stay up all night while fasting to perform spiritual practices such as mantra chanting and kirtan (musical mantra chanting). Then, at around 3 a.m. all the monks and attendees would stride in ceremonious musical procession to the sacred River Ganga and take baths before returning for the final rituals and breaking fast. Performing Ekadashi with such spiritual vigor is outrageously uplifting, yet still you can get a powerful boost by doing a simpler version with fasting and a little meditation at home.

To practice Ekadashi, eat only fruits and vegetables, avoid grains, and do extra meditation. Doing this is one of the best things for your physical, mental, and spiritual well-being.

Mantra: Lam. If you really want to balance a particular element you may chant its mantra for some time during meditation, but honestly I don't recommend it with much enthusiasm. There are much more powerful mantras that you could chant instead. These go right to the soul and are conveniently sprinkled throughout this book.

Affirmation: I am structured, straightforward, and clear. (Affirmations like this are not Vedic, but they can be helpful, so I have included one for each element. You can use this to imbibe the quality of the element you want more of.)

Water

Water is soft, fluid, flowing, and adaptable. Water is the tender healer that calms, cools, and brings harmony. Water holds no firm agenda. It is most known for its changeable nature: It takes the shape of its container and can become hard as ice or as soft as clouds. Water nourishes and causes growth; it is like the soothing mother that nurtures her loved ones to grow powerful and strong.

Qualities: Adaptable, changing, fluid, cooling, flexible, emotional, psychic, spiritual, compassionate, intuitive, nourishing, feminine, creative, deep, sensual, sexual.

Negative Qualities: Volatile, fickle, moody, sensitive, temperamental.

Dharma of Water: Water is best understood when we understand its nature is twofold. On one hand, water is uneasy and characterized by turmoil and turbulence, like the tumultuous waves of the sea; and on the other hand water strives for peace, for harmony, and for tranquility like a peacefully serene river or lake. Despite this dual nature, water is biased to its calm and tender nature. Water's purpose is to nourish and support life as well as to bring flavor and feeling to any situation. Earth can be boring. Water makes the stiffness of earth interesting by providing variety and flavor, for water is all about taste, flavor, and fun. Water soothes the burn and uneasiness caused by excess fire.

Visual: The gracious nourishing mother that is also a free-spirited, dancing, emotional healer.

Quantity in Existence: There is more water than earth in existence. This is easily seen when we look at our planet: There are more oceans than land, even though it is land that provides the borders that contain the oceans. In our bodies there is more water than earth, which means more fluid than solid.

What to Use Water For: Increase the water element when you are looking for flavor, fun, healing, and also when you want a variety of options and the best possible thing to act on. Increase water when you need to be soothed tenderly and calmed from the stresses of life. Use water to nourish and slide through life. You can increase the energy of water by imbibing the qualities of water like being soft, intuitive, and most importantly adaptable.

Examples

THE LIFE OF THE PARTY

If there is a rigid boring social event, like an office party, that needs some fun or you just want to be the life of a party, imbibe the free spirit of water. Flow between people, socializing with them while maintaining empathy and gentleness; this is the energy of water and it will not-so-metaphorically "stir things up." Move and encourage others to move, as water moves. This can be through dancing, though even just having people move around the room will get things going.

EFFECTIVE IN BUSINESS

In Chapter 12 we will go into the exact process of how to create things with maximum effectiveness, but in short, be flexible if you want tangible results. Flexibility creates solidity. Creation happens from subtle to physical, so water, which is flexibility, comes just before earth in the continuum of the elements and therefore it is essential to be adaptable like water to get tangible results, which are in earth's domain.

To bring the power of water to a business, change things up to keep employees feeling good. Be tender and intuitive when communicating with customers, employees, and suppliers. Adapt to the market, which means being in tune with the ever-changing emotions of the marketplace.

Water is sensitive to emotions, and emotions are what drive market consumption. By increasing water energy, you will become more in tune with the feelings of the market and can adjust your brand, products, and processes to meet the changing wants and feelings of your market.

In Relationships

Water is a very relational element, so the common advice of being sensitive, tender, soft, and empathetic is part of the water element in a relationship. If you want harmony, don't be too earth-like and stubborn; adapt and flow with your partner's feelings, needs, and wants, and peace and harmony will prevail. Yet be careful: If you have too much water energy in a relationship and lack the backbone-like structure of earth that provides (such as clear boundaries, schedules, goals, etc.), then the negatives of water can take over, and the relationship can become unpredictable, intense, and full of turmoil, confusion, drama, and chaos just like the waves of the ocean during a storm.

In Health

Water is carefree. This is the energy needed to decrease stress caused by the passionate and ambitious fire. Stress is one of the most detrimental things to health. This has not only been proven with scientific studies of the stress hormones cortisol and adrenaline, but has also been well understood by holistic doctors for thousands of years. Therefore one tip to improve your health is to spend some time relaxing with no agenda and, like water, flow with where the "Universe takes you." This could mean a meandering walk in the park or imbibing the energy of water through dance. Whatever it is that sets you free to move your body and flow with feeling, do that, and the tranquil, tender healing of water will sooth your pain.

Water Activities

Some of the things you can do that are very water-like and will increase the energy of this element in you are: flowy tai chi, painting, dance, music, massage, and even some forms of jujitsu. You can even ask a yoga teacher for poses for the second chakra.

Extras for Water

In Medicine: Kidneys and urinary bladder.
Chakra: 2nd, Swadhisthana.
Astrology: Venus, Moon, Jupiter and Cancer/Scorpio/Pisces.
Sense Object: Taste.
Knowledge Acquiring Sense: Tongue.
Mantra: Vam.
Affirmation: I feel, adapt, and flow.

Fire

Fire is a fantastic element filled with flare, power, life, and vigor. Fire is motivation, drive, passion, and the forceful energy that actually gets things done. Fire is not only what makes things happen, it is what gives the spark of style and beauty. Fire is the consumer and to satisfy its passions and whims it will not hesitate to use anything in its wake. With high power comes high risk. Fire can power factories, fuel nations, and create amazing shiny things, yet it can also be the insatiable unsatisfied flames of an undying forest fire. The unsatisfied greed of fire can wreak havoc by destroying economies, relationships, companies, and nations. If fire is tempered by the healing tranquility of water and fueled by the condensed energy of air it is unstoppable and will create all that is fabulous, fancy, and fun.

Qualities: Driven, passionate, motivated, visionary, dominant, eager, productive, fast, flamboyant, stylish, sensational, high-energy, intense, undeniably noticeable, expansive, joyful, enthusiastic, sexy, heat, light, color, inspiration, charisma, mystery (you never know what is behind the flames or what they will do). Fire is clarity.

Negative Qualities: Greedy, fickle, self-destructive, dangerous.

Dharma: Fire is characterized by intense passion. Its strong energy strives to enjoy and to consume. These desires are what drive it to action and therefore can be incredibly productive, yet if there is not enough energy for it to consume, it fizzles out. Thus it needs constant stimulation. If you ever looked into a flame you have seen that it is beautiful, attractive, and shiny. Looks matter *a lot* to it, as it is the very element that brings the ability to see into the world.

Visual: A king living in a fancy palace managing his nation while conquering others. In modern times, rich and powerful entrepreneurs or CEOs are the icon of the fire element.

What to Use Fire For: Increase the fire element when you need passion, drive, or motivation. If you want to bring flash, flare, and style to a situation, fire is your element. When something needs to get done, you can count on fire to find a way.

Examples

Looking Good and Getting Attention

Nothing grabs attention like fire. If you want to be the star of the moment, use the fire's flare. Wear flashy colors; put on something that sparkles and shines. Move and speak with passion. Intentionally exude a bright vibrant intensity, and look at people with a bright, piercing gaze. Medically speaking (Ayurveda), the eyes are predominated by the fire element and in the Vedic approach sight is the sense that correlates with fire, so you can always spot a passionately driven and inspired person through their eyes. Be that person and you will command the attention of the room, for fire equals charisma.

Effective in Business

Fire is what motivates many people to start businesses. Fire's drive, vision, and passion are what brought your business to life in the first place. Be careful and don't let that fire dwindle; keep the dream alive! Don't let the negatives of fire take prominence by letting the passion fizzle out or by being overly aggressive and burning your surroundings. Sustainable inspiration can be maintained not only by reviewing your motivation to kindle the fire of your vision, but also by inspiring and infecting others with your passion—catching them on fire—so they also burn with the same excitement that fuels your vision. When all partners and employees are motivated with the same vision then they must and will obliterate everything in their path to make your project or company a smashing success, for fire-like people are unstoppable and the most success-driven.

To effectively ignite your vision in your team, adopt the shine and charisma of fire. Rather than just adopting almost superficial shine, let true charisma, in the form of your inspiration, clear vision, and passion, shine through you. If your passion is strong enough it will ooze out of you and ignite any dry kindle (person with the potential to also burn with your vision) in the vicinity.

Watch out: Make sure there is enough fuel to keep the fire going. Fire eats a lot of energy and needs the raw energy of the air element (which not-so-coincidentally comes before fire in the elemental spectrum) to keep it going.

In Relationships

There is no doubt that fire in the form of passion is key in a relationship. Fire can be present in a relationship in two ways. The first is in the form of a partnership in which both members are motivated and driven with the same purpose and vision. If this is the case, make sure that you are both burning with the same intensity; having one person less motivated for the shared vision than the other will lead to disharmony. Align your visions: One large fire encompassing both of you is better than two separate fires burning next to each other. Of course there are plenty of beautiful and successful relationships in which each party is motivated by something different, but the most intensely inspiring relationships are when the couple burns as one. This unity of souls, passion, and vision is what is most satisfying in relationships. This is the intense harmony that many of us strive for.

If you are in a relationship that does not have such like-minded visionary flare and you would like to create one, then make sure that one partner's fire is strong enough to ignite the other partner and that the to-be-ignited partner has the potential to be ignited. This potential exists in two ways:

1. As sufficient amounts of raw energy (air element) to sustain the consuming fire of passion. It takes energy to execute a

vision, and you must feel you have the energy to actually manifest the vision to truly be passionate about it.

2. As "dry kindle," meaning that the to-be-ignited partner must be ready to be ignited for the vision and be like-minded enough to be motivated by such a vision. Not everyone can be ignited for every vision. We all have our own dharma and preferences and thus can only truly be inspired by certain visions or goals. Even if we have the potential to be inspired by a particular vision, we must also be mature enough and in the right phase of our life for the flame to really catch us. A child will not be inspired for a woman in the same way as an adult, and a teenager may not be inspired for a business in the same way as an older person. Therefore it is fundamentally important to pick a compatible partner with similar tastes and interests if you want to burn together in productive passionate action.

Sexual Passion

The next way in which fire permeates a relationship is in sexual passion. Fire is beauty and attractiveness; when one shines with the beauty of fire people are attracted. Oftentimes a person's beauty is hidden; it is covered like a secret hot coal and only in a deep and connected relationship are those hidden coals seen. Whether one's beauty is hidden or overt, sexual and relational passion happens when someone sees the fire of attractiveness in their lover and the fire of desire to savor that beauty ignites in their heart.

The most passionate relationships are when such fire of desire has ignited in both lovers' hearts and they both yearn and passionately strive to savor each other. When these four fires meet—each individual's fire of desire and each one's fire of attractiveness—there is an explosion of passion, and the connection and sex are superbly intense.

By nature, fire is changing and the mysterious flames of such a relationship lead the couple to new adventures and pleasures. Fire is the showman and thus this quadruple-lit relationship is never shy of drama.

These intense relationships seldom last because such a strong fire burns fuel quickly. To keep such relationships lit you must continue to feed them with novelty, as well as make sure to keep the desire in each lover's heart lit.

Separation makes the heart grow fonder; undesired distance in a relationship makes the heart yearn more. Therefore bouts of distance and separation are keys to maintaining a highly passionate and intense relationship, for once the object of desire is fully attained, the fire of lust has no new fuel to burn, mystery and novelty are lost, and the fire fizzles out. Therefore, create some distance and introduce unpredictable novelty if you wish to keep your relationship passionately on fire.

One-Sided Obsession

One-sided obsessive fires are common and easily understood. This happens when one partner shines brighter than the other and the "dimmer" partner yearns for the warmth and beauty of the brighter one. If you are the person who is attracted to another and they are not attracted to you, show not only your shine, but your shiny qualities that will inspire the fire of lust in your loved one's heart. Tune into their needs, wants, and fantasies, and imbibe these qualities they seek. If you have no such qualities, get them, or give up and find someone else who values the shiny beauty you have to offer.

IN HEALTH

Fire's role in health is of fundamental importance. People refer to "the fire of digestion." Fire takes in raw energy and processes it to make it useful. Food has energy, but that energy can only be used once fire has digested it and transformed it into usable energy in the body. There are many foods that are too dense to be processed by the fire of digestion alone, so we cook them first and let external fires do the initial processing. Therefore to have bountiful amounts of energy, simply eating well is not enough: We must also have a powerful fire of digestion so that we are able to absorb its nutrients.

Cook with ginger to enhance the digestive fire. Chinese cooking often uses big chunks of ginger for this reason. Chilis, on the other hand, also increase fire, but the "wrong" type of fire that can aggravate the body and unhealthily burn energy rather then gently supporting the digestive fire the way ginger does.

Do not drink anything for at least 30 to 45 minutes after eating; this kills the digestive fire. Ice cream and other cold foods are fun but are harmful to digestive fire, so enjoy these in moderation.

During my 18 years in India I met one of the best Ayurvedic doctors in the land, Dr. Raju. He is famous and has treated hundreds of thousands of patients. I was amazed in his nearly magical ability to read pulses. He explained that one of the healthiest things you can do is to simply sip hot water. As I traveled the world, I noticed that in China everyone almost always only drank hot water. When you stay at someone's house, you receive a large flask with hot water, the public water fountains are hot water fountains, and it is actually hard to find cold drinking water anywhere. Hot water aids the fire of digestion, and these ancient cultures know it. Power your digestion by developing the habit of drinking hot water or herbal teas.

Another important way the fire element exists in the body is in physical exertion. When you move and exercise, the fire element is increased and your body temperature rises so much that water drips from your body as sweat. (Fire comes before water in the elemental spectrum, and thus fire creates water.) Calories are burned, and more importantly fire does what it does best: converts raw energy into assimilated and useable power. Through the process of exercise fire turns food and air into muscle.

With Great Power Comes Great Responsibility

Fire is powerful and can be used in many wonderful ways, only some of which I described here, but be careful, my dear friend: Excess fire can burn badly and cause tremendous harm. It is important to know that fire, being more subtle than earth and water, takes on many forms. Electricity is fire, light is fire, the sun is fire, digestion is fire, body heat is fire, and friction is fire. Some types of fire are more conducive for certain actions than others, and the wrong type of fire can wreak havoc. We like and need fire in our homes; we use it to keep us warm, to cook, and to let us see, but a flaming fire that we may enjoy on a camping trip can destroy our home, especially if it gets too big. In the same way a strong digestive fire can be the best thing for our health, too much heat in the body can cause a multitude of ailments. Foods such as chilis, pickles, sugar, tomatoes, and even fried food can cause the wrong type of heat in the body, whereas ginger, cumin, anise, radish, and simply warm food can cause the right type. Foods that cool an excess of fire in the body are things like fresh fruits and vegetables, especially cucumbers.

> ### Chinese Grandmothers
>
> If you work up a sweat every day you will feel great and your health with flourish. Walking after a meal generates the right type of fire and aids digestion. Some grandmothers in China told me that if you walk 99 steps after eating you will live for 99 years. I then asked, "What if I want to live more than 99 years?" They replied that 99 just means "a lot" in the Chinese culture.

Again I reiterate that there are entire medical sciences based on the elements and if you have an ailment or want to know more, find a qualified doctor. I recommend seeing a good Chinese acupuncturist or Chinese herbalist, for I have found that they have best preserved the wisdom and application of the elements in their health systems. Ayurvedic doctors are also great. It is worthy to note that there is reasonable historical evidence to support the idea that acupuncture and other Chinese health systems originated in India, in the Ayurveda, and were then transported to China by Buddhist monks. A book called *The Lost Secrets of Ayurvedic Acupuncture* by Dr. Frank Ros explains this in detail and also explains how the Vedic and Chinese system of the elements are pretty much the same.

ON THE SPIRITUAL PATH

A common myth about the spiritually enlightened is that they are artificially meek and hide their light from the world. Though true humility is a natural and fundamentally important part of the spiritual process, a true spiritualist is a giver who allows their light to shine and uses it in the service of others. When you perform spiritual practices, like the ones outlined in this book, an effulgent light can begin to shine from you. This is a very sweet side of the fire element. If you are fortunate to have such light exude from you, do not hide it, for it is rooted in your spiritual inspiration, passion, and clarity. Use it to help others to also progress on their spiritual path. *Light* is a fundamental part of the en*light*end, so shine on.

Watch out, though: If you think this light is yours and that people are attracted to you because of you alone, your false ego is probably becoming unhealthily big. It may blind you and you may lose sight of your own spiritual path. History is littered with the corpses of spiritual leaders who took their followers' worship and praise for themselves, and forgot that the source of their attractiveness was a supremely sweet superior power beyond them.

Fire Activities: Vision boards, pep talks, war cries, motivational seminars, charismatic speeches like the famous "I Have a Dream" speech by Dr. Martin Luther King, Hakka dances as well as sensual dancing such as salsa. Working out, certain types of yogic pranayam breathing, and martial arts beautifully increase fire. And of course, you can always do yoga exercises for the 3rd chakra.

Extras for Fire

In Medicine: Heart, Small intestines.
Chakra: 3nd Chakra, Manipura.
Mantra: Ram (Rang).
Astrology: Sun and Mars, and Aries/Leo/Sagittarius.
Sense Object: Sight.
Knowledge Acquiring Sense: Eyes.
Affirmation: I want, I do.

CHAPTER 7

THE POWER OF AIR—
PRANA—CHI

We are now getting even more into the subtle realm, which means we shall more deeply uncover the immense power that is hidden to most people's eyes.

Air Is Power

You cannot see air, yet without it you will die. If you need to lift something heavy, you hold your breath because it is the power of air that strengthens you. When you are doing strenuous work or working out, your breath will hasten because raw power lies in the air element. Ask any successful athlete, martial artist, or yoga master, and they will attest that controlling your breath is key in effectively and successfully mastering their art, for it is in your breath that extraordinary power lies. Control your breath to control your physical and mental vigor.

The God of Air in Hindu Theology/Mythology

The Hindu theology believes that each of the various forces in nature has different managerial Lords. Some call these beings Gods or demigods.

We understand that rather than Gods, they are more like employees assigned by the Supreme to be responsible for and manage a particular area of the Universe. Each of them presides over and controls the particular function they are responsible for. Whether these "Gods" exist or not is not the discussion for the moment. Believing in the possibility of their existence really depends on your beliefs about the world and your faith. For now, whether you see their existence as fact or myth, you can still extract much wisdom about the way the world works by looking at the stories of these "Gods."

The "God" of air is named Vayu, and he is the strongest and most powerful. There are stories about when someone basically ticked him off and he stopped allowing anyone to breathe until the culprit redeemed himself; there are tales of his incarnations carrying mountains; and so forth. These tales yet again emphasize the vital point that in air is where strength lies.

More Subtle, More Powerful, More Dangerous

When I was a teenager in the monastery and we were studying yoga and jujitsu, our teacher had us do many intense exercises as well as many fancy and tough yoga poses, yet he would not teach us or lets us do pranayama. Pranayama is a type of yoga exercise that is about controlling the breath. It is not strenuous; it is simply a type of breathing. Though apparently simple, it is actually high-level yoga and for the majority of the time it was too high a level for us. Every week, in our martial arts classes, we would do full-contact, no-holds-barred sparring. This was safe for us to do, but pranayama breathing techniques? Oh no, they were too dangerous.

How does this make sense? Everybody breathes all the time, so what would be the harm if we were to practice these breathing techniques? The reason for all the caution was because the air element is enormously powerful and, just like fire, if you don't channel it properly it can be extremely dangerous. The more subtle the element, the more powerful, and air is more powerful than fire or any of the previous elements.

Air Is Prana or Chi

When I am referring to air, I am not just referring to the air that we breathe and that is blown by fans. The domain of the air element also includes an elusive force known as prana or, as the Chinese call it, chi. For those who are not familiar with this amazing substance, prana or chi is the subtle vital living energy that permeates all things. Prana is life force; without it there cannot be life. There is an ancient Chinese proverb that says we can live for three weeks without food, three days without water, and three minutes without air, but we cannot live for even three seconds without chi.

Prana or chi flows through the body and when it is blocked or deficient, disease is certain. The entire process of hatha yoga is simply about increasing this prana energy in the body and having it flow properly. The health system of Ayurveda is also simply designed to align this energy so that it flows properly within the body. The entire acupuncture system is about locating in which organs or energy channels this energy is blocked, and then unblocking it with the use of needles or moxa.

Tai chi and other martial arts are all about channeling this energy in combat. The shaolin monks that break iron bars on their heads and withstand the piercing of spears and even power drills against their bare skin do it all by the control of this elusive, invisible, and astronomically powerful force: chi, prana, or the air element.

The unbendable arm technique, which you learned in a previous chapter, works because it channels and focuses this air energy.

Those who don't breathe are dead, and those who breathe shallowly and are deficient in energy are dying faster than the rest of us. Master the air element, and weakness and lack of energy will not be your problem.

Our Two Bodies

The Vedas explain that you are a living entity, a spirit soul that is covered by the eight elements. They explain that the eight elements take the form of two bodies: the physical body and the subtle body. The physical body is made of the first five elements: earth, water, fire, air, and ether; the subtle body is composed of the three subtle elements: the mind, intelligence, and false ego. Later we will go more in depth about understanding these bodies and their importance for our own personal empowerment and our spiritual path to passionate enlightenment. I bring up the concept of these two bodies here because in addition to these two bodies there is another type of subtle body that is predominantly composed of the air element. Some people call this body the etheric body or energy body.

Energy medicine systems such as acupuncture, Ayurveda, and jin sin jitsu primarily work on this energy body because it is understood that the physical body that we can touch and see follows suit to this energy body. According to these systems, if there is an ailment in the energy body it will become physical, and the physical cannot be fully healthy until the energy body is healed.

The Energy Body

This energy body is composed of subtle vein-like energy pathways that flow throughout our entire physical body. In Sanskrit these pathways are called nadis and there are 72,000 of them. They bring air/prana/chi to every bone, organ, and cell of your body. Fourteen of these nadis, which correlate to particular organs, have been singled out and are used for the system of acupuncture. Three of these nadis (Ida, Pingala, and Sushumna) start at the base of the spine and span to the top of the head; they criss-cross along the way and create spirals of energy that become the powerful energy centers in the body known as chakras. All of these energy channels and chakras vibrate energy to create the aura, which are claimed to be felt and sometimes seen by the subtly attuned.

What I just explained about the energy body is fascinating for many people but it is not fundamentally important to know for spiritual growth or for basic effectiveness, so don't worry if it is confusing or not fully understood at the moment. I briefly described this energy body for two reasons. First, for people who are familiar with and deal with the energy body, it is helpful for them to know where it fits on the continuum of the elements. Second, it is helpful to know that you have such an energy body. By being aware of it you will be able to make micro adjustments in your habits that will prove fruitful. Some of the tips given in this book will make more sense when you know about the energy body, and when you come across advice in life a lot of it will make more sense when you are aware of the energy body.

A technical note: This energy body that is made of the air element is technically still the physical body. The air element is still much denser and physical than the true subtle elements of mind, intelligence, and false ego. I have called this energy body a separate body because in the west we are not used to acknowledging and interacting with air/prana/chi energy or this energy body in our daily habits. In the East, however, it is normal to make diet and other choices based on the energy body and its needs and functions. It is not uncommon for an Indian to say, "I will eat yogurt to cool my stomach fire" or for a Chinese person to say, "I will eat white radish to increase my lung chi."

In any case, air is a fundamentally powerful element that entire sciences, even those beyond health and medical systems, such as Vastu, feng shui, and Chi Gong, are rooted in.

Air Is Raw Power

Air is raw energy. It is this raw power that fire needs to act and create with. If you want power and efficacy in the world you must have high energy, which means you must have sufficient amounts of the air element in your being so that fire can transmute it into practical action, for fire burns air. When people speak of energy, they are actually referring to this air element. Let's explore this element a little further so that we can extract practical and cool gems of wisdom to make us more effective and ease our path to Passionate Enlightenment.

Qualities: Pure, strong, swift, hidden, grave, mature, all pervading, nourishing, compliant, supportive, energetic, moving, physicality (the sense of touch is related to the air element), nourishing, pleasure, vigor, mystery.

Negative Qualities: Volatile, changing, can cause major destruction if contaminated or not flowing properly.

Dharma of Air: The Dharma or duty of air is to bring life. In the Sanskrit language the words for "air," "energy," and "life" are the exact same word: *prana*. If there is no air there is no life. Air is constantly flowing and in its movement it gives life. By breathing in and out, the life energy of air enters your body and keeps you alive. Just as the physical aspect of the air element, oxygen, flows through your veins and reaches every part of your body, keeping you alive and full of energy, the subtle part of the air element, the prana or chi, also travels through the vein-like energy channels in your body (known as meridians or nadis), bringing life and energy to every part of your body.

The movement of air around the planet cross-pollinates plants, allowing their species to survive, and the most pleasurable and invigorating part of human procreation (sex) is when the air energy moves and intertwines through both lovers' bodies. Orgasm happens when air energy moves. The ancient and sophisticated sexual practices of the East, such as Kama Sutra, Tantra, and Taoist sex, can last for hours, multiply pleasure, and invigorate the body, and are all about properly channeling and flowing with the air element. For it is desire, power, and pleasure that defines life; air is life.

Air/prana permeates all living things, infusing them with its living force, for air/prana is the living force of life.

Touch and feel are in the domain of air, so the pleasure of feeling exists in the air element, as opposed to the pleasure of tasting, which is in the domain of the water element.

Visual: An electric current shooting through wires powering your computer, your house, your entire city, and the rest of the world.

Examples

EFFECTIVE IN BUSINESS/PROJECT

As described when we were speaking about fire, air is raw energy, and you need to make sure there is enough of its energy to fuel your project or it will not survive. Your business is like a living organism and needs the constant influx of energy to keep it alive. Just as breath keeps the body alive, in

the same way things that imbibe the principle of the air element will keep
your business alive. And just as you need to keep breathing there needs to
be a constant inflow of these air-like things in your business or project.
Things that represent the air element for your business or project are:

1. Money. Most businesses fail and most fail due to underfund-
    ing; this is a statistical fact. When raising capital raise more
    than you think you need to ensure there is enough energy to
    keep the business alive or for starting the fire of a new proj-
    ect or business. Expanding an existing business or starting a
    new business can consume more than you expect.

    Air is movement, and *cash flow* is the single most impor-
    tant phrase in business. You must learn to manage it if you
    want to stay successful. There are entire books and courses on
    cash-flow management; study them if you do not have this skill
    yet. In essence, there must be a greater influx of money (air)
    than what the business (fire) consumes. Of course, this sounds
    simple, to make more money than you spend, but surprisingly
    many businesses do not do this. That's why business mogul
    Warren Buffett says, "Rule No. 1: Never lose money. Rule No.
    2: Never forget rule No.1" and "You only have to do a very few
    things right in your life so long as you don't do too many things
    wrong." Just as managing breath ensures the life of the body,
    managing cash flow ensures the life of your business or project.

2. Customers. It may be obvious to say that you need customers,
    but a few steady customers are not enough. Don't lose per-
    spective of the importance of constantly breathing in new cus-
    tomers. Your business is weak and runs the risk of dying fast if
    you depend on only a few customers. Just as your body needs
    a constant intake of air, your business needs a constant intake
    of customers. Just as you breathe deeply and take more air in
    when working out to expand the size of your muscles, you need
    to take more customers in to expand the size of your business.
    If you only have limited customers and are not growing that
    number, a change in your current customer's organizational
    policy or need could speak death to your business or project.

3. Innovations. Yes, the steadiness of earth is extremely valuable for a business, and the aphorism "If it ain't broke, don't fix it" still stands strong in unwavering truth. But innovation, in process, in products, and in marketing, is essential if your business is to stand the test of time. So many companies have become obsolete; don't be one of them. Innovate to sustain a competitive edge. Fire is inspiration and motivation, and the novelty of innovation is the air, which it needs to stay aflame.

Air energy needs to flow, and to keep your mind fresh, innovative, and powerful, your workspace must be supportive. Energy must be able to flow in it. Feng shui and Vastu are not just ancient architectural systems only meant to make pretty buildings. These are systems that can be used to set up your physical environment so that energy properly flows in it, and so that it is conducive for the activity you are performing (in this case, thinking and working). If you are extremely serious hire a Vastu or feng shui expert to set up your workspace in a way to support your creativity and productivity. If you're not ready to hire someone, keep your environment as decluttered as possible, make sure there is good ventilation, and keep it clean, so the air element can flow in your space. Keep in mind that the air element is purity. A proper environment can really do wonders for your ability to think.

An air-related thing you can do if you need to think is to go for a walk outside. By moving your body, prana/chi/air can flow in it, and by walking outside, you can absorb the prana/chi/life force from nature. I find that new ideas come easily and I can much more easily solve tough problems with the fresh air/prana/chi and oxygen flowing in my body and brain.

Exercise for Using the Principle of Air in a Project

Make a list of all air-like things that are needed in your project to keep it afloat and growing. What things other than capital, innovations, and customers are needed as a constant influx of supportive energy that your project or business will die without (e.g., social media shares, events booked, calls made, hours worked, sleep, and so forth)?

Do whatever you need to make sure these things are available.

IN RELATIONSHIPS

In the section on fire I explained that a fire-like passionate relationship needs constant fuel to stay on fire. The air-like fuel that keep relationships going are things such as novelty, mystery, affection, and the satisfaction of desires. Fire is passion and has many wants; air is the hidden force—the secret energy that is the ability to fulfill these desires. This can be in the form of time, money, and other forms of wealth such as a house, nice clothes, or a hotel room. My friend, here is an example of what this means, because I know these concepts can be quite esoteric and confusing at times: The fire-like inspiration in a relationship inspires both lovers to go on a romantic vacation together. This vacation can only happen if they have the time, money, and health to do so. In this case the time, money, and health are the air element, the raw energy needed to fulfill the inspiration of this fire-like vacation. Simply said, you need the money to do what you want. The more air energy in the relationship, the more the inspiration and passion of fire can last and flourish. Many relationships suffer because of lack of money (air).

Also, physical health is required for good sex; physical health, vigor, and energy are air. When a man ejaculates he loses a large amount of prana/chi/energy or air, and because of the loss of this energy the sex dies down or ends. Men often feel very weak and drained when they ejaculate. Therefore, for the best sex, men must learn to control their prana/chi/air element by learning to control their ejaculation and thus make sex a rejuvenating, energizing experience, rather than a depleting and destructive one.

The air element is more significant than just the fuel for fire. Air has no borders and flows between things, connecting them in an invisible way.

The Highest Expression of Love

Sometimes people wonder why I always speak of romantic relationships when I am writing or teaching about relationships. In life we have so many other types of relationships: friends, family, coworkers, business relationships, and even social media relationships. Romantic relationships are just one type of relationship. My reason for this is that the ancient Vedic wisdom goes into exquisite depth on the nature of relationships. It is understood that the most important and fundamental parts of life lies in good relationships; there are many large Vedic texts simply on the nature of relationship. Spiritual growth and enlightenment are all about creating a passionate relationship with the divine. Vedic wisdom, and perhaps our own experiences, tells us that the highest expression of love and relationship is a romantic one. These relationships are the most intense, inspiring, deep, and fulfilling. In a sense, relationships are one: A relationship is a relationship, but the difference between them, aside from the individuality of the persons involved, is the intensity. So a relationship with an acquaintance is the same as a relationship with your spouse; all the same principles of relationship apply, but the depth, closeness, flavor, and intensity create a world of difference. For all relationships you must be polite, caring, communicative, purposeful, and so forth, and use all the principles of the elements that I am describing here. Therefore when I talk about romantic relationships, all other relationships are included in that. These are just anecdotal examples for you to understand the elements and begin to learn how to use them.

In Yoga and on the Spiritual Path

Yoga has become extremely popular in the Western world. Though people know that yoga provides immense physical and even psychological benefits, they often forget that yoga is primarily a spiritual practice. The core difference between yoga and other exercise is that yoga, being an integrated holistic systems, also works on the energy body—the body that is composed of the air element known as prana or chi. Each yoga posture is designed to clear and balance the prana in particular parts of the body. When this subtle air energy is flowing correctly and is thus healthy, the physical body must also follow suit and be healthy and powerful. Anyone who knows about yoga with any significance knows this. They know that both the energy body and physical body are intertwined, and that yoga works on both. However, what is not so commonly known is that the mind rests on the energy body. If the energy body is disturbed the mind will also be disturbed. That is why people often feel so peaceful and calm, and can focus easily after a good yoga session.

For the energy body to be in balance the physical body must also be. What yoga does is work on the physical body so that the energy body can come into balance. And in sequence, yoga works on the energy body so that the mind can come into balance. When the mind is in balance, one can meditate; and the highest most potent form of meditation, which is imbued with sweetness, is meditation on the Divine, especially when the heart is filled with love.

I mention this now to iterate the point that for a focused mind we must control and balance the air element. I also deeply want you to understand that a focused mind is one of the most classically powerful tools helpful for ascending to Enlightenment. But remember: The fullest realms of bliss, which are a natural side effect of Passionate Enlightenment, are beyond all the elements and can only be fully attained when you heart is full of sincere love and you spiritually surrender 100 percent of your being to the beauty of the divine.

Quick Tip

1. Meditate after yoga for your meditation to be more powerful.
2. Do pranayama before mediation to balance the air element.
3. Do a meditation that vibrates air (Mantra Meditation).

Air Activities: Anything that gets you moving is a key to increasing, supporting, and purifying the air element. When air is flowing it is the best. So any type of sport, dance, stretching, or exercise is good for toning the air element. There are specific systems that work with the air element, such as yoga, chi gong, tai chi, and pranayama, and I highly recommend them. Massage and acupuncture also work wonders in getting the energy to flow in your body.

Air is life force and exists everywhere, especially in nature, so getting in touch with nature helps the air element absorb into your body. It is best if you can connect with a variety of nature's facets, such as oceans, mountains, and forests. This way you can absorb different qualities of energy provided by the different facets of nature.

Air Energy and Food: Food is one of the main sources of prana for the body. Eat a variety of food. Fresh food such as fruits and vegetables provide the most easily assimilated form of energy, whereas old and processed foods have less energy, because the air or prana disperses with time. Interestingly, though, Mother Nature has found a way to condense and store large amounts of energy in seeds and grains, which can be stored for a long time without losing their prana. Seeds need this energy to have the power to grow into a plant. Meat, on the other hand, not only loses its energy fast, it is also filled with the negative energy of death that is destructive for both the body and the mind. The spiritual Gurus of ancient India clearly state you can never enter into the deepest and best states of meditation and clear focus if your physical body, energy body, and mind are permeated by the negative and harsh energy of dead animals in your system. For this reason, as well as to increase the qualities of compassion and to avoid the bad karma of killing, a vegetarian diet is recommended on the spiritual path.

Extras for Air

In Medicine: Lung, large intestines.
Chakra: 4th, heart, Anahata.
Astrology: Mercury and Gemini/Libra/Aquarius.
Sense Object: Touch.
Knowledge Acquiring Sense: Skin.
Mantra: Yam.
Affirmation: I flow with purity, power, and pleasure.

CHAPTER 8

THE SERENITY OF ETHER

Ether is the midpoint between the subtle and the physical elements. Though it is considered a physical element, it is like a gateway that gives us access to the actual subtle domain. As mentioned before, English words don't accurately communicate these ancient ideas and concepts, which were originally taught in the Sanskrit language. Some people prefer to call this element sky, sound, or space. These words are also okay, but I will call it ether for simplicity even though, scientifically speaking, the ether element, as defined in the scientific community, does not exist. I use the word *ether* as a signpost to convey the concept of this element.

Ether Exists in 2 Forums

1. Space

All physical things exist somewhere. They reside in the subtle, invisible, and elusive element known as ether or space. Just as all fish reside in the water, all physical things—or more specifically, all the other four physical elements—reside in ether.

There are some knowledge systems that only expound upon the first four elements: earth, water, fire, and air. I think this is because the more subtle elements, such as ether, are less tangible and harder to perceive than the more subtle ones.

The ether element is so subtle that if you move a physical object—a rock, for example—the ether element remains unmoved and practically unaffected, unlike the four other physical elements, which will be affected by such an action. Just as moving a net in air does not affect the air due to the large holes that allow the finer substance of air to remain unmoved, ether or space is not moved when the other denser elements move.

2. Sound

Another fundamentally important aspect of the ether element is sound. This is perhaps less abstract and easier to perceive than viewing ether as space or sky.

An untrained mind may think that sound is created by physical things such as vocal cords, engines, or musical instruments, but in truth, sound, just like space, exists everywhere. If you clap your hands or tap a wall you will find sound, for sound is everywhere.

The questions are: How and in what state does sound/ether exist? When it is not audible? And what does it matter for us on our quest for effective action and/or Passionate Enlightenment? Here is where things get really interesting, but before we dive into it, I must warn you that we are getting extremely subtle here, which means things will be *a lot* harder to perceive. It is easy to understand and grasp the concepts of the physical elements, as they are by nature much more visible as measurable and tangible. But to understand and perceive the more subtle elements takes a much more sensitive, intuitive, and subtly attuned mind that frankly most people don't have. It takes practice and training to perceive these superfine and subtle aspects of reality. Therefore, when we start to deliberate on these subjects it may seem woo-woo or imaginary to some, but for the subtly attuned, this knowledge system makes so much sense, because interacting with, seeing, and perceiving these more subtle things are a normal part of their life. Knowledge of this element has been used to win wars and manage entire empires. Powerful business executives have used such wisdom. This is not the wisdom only meant for the use of mystical hermits that have no need for effective practical life, this wisdom is best suited for those who have large responsibilities in the world and who must have the best and most accurate knowledge to be successful.

Back to the questions: In what state does sound/ether exist when it is not audible, and how can knowledge of the ether element help us on our quest for effective action and/or Passionate Enlightenment? The 5,000-year-old wisdom of Veda tells us that all-pervading sound vibration exists as a micro vibration that is within all things. This micro vibration is the ether element. When some people study reality from a scientific standpoint, they come to the conclusion that everything is actually just a vibration. This conclusion is similar to, and touches upon, the concept of the ether element. When they look deeply into subatomic particles, such as protons, neutrons, quarks, and so forth, they find that they are either vibrating or they are a vibration (science does not really know which it is yet) and from this they understand that in essence everything is just a vibration. They see that different physical objects can simply be seen as different types of vibrations. So one way in which we can understand the ether or sound element is as a hidden sound vibration that not only exists everywhere and within everything but that all things are simply different permutations of this ether/sound vibration.

Let's go into more depth and uncover the mysteries hidden within this superb knowledge system.

The existence of prana or air depends on the existence of this subtle "ether" vibration. This is a normal trend in this Unprecedented Elemental Reality System. The more physical elements depend on the more subtle elements that come before them in the sequence. Fire depends on air: If there is no air then fire cannot exist. That's why if you light a candle and put it in an airtight container, the fire will die once the air has been consumed. In the same way, water in its proper fluid form cannot exist without fire; with no fire water becomes ice. Earth also cannot exist without water. Solid things cannot remain solid unless there is fluid to bind them; physical solid things would disintegrate into micro dust if there was no water element.

With this understanding a very interesting notion comes to light: Energy/prana/chi depends on and is controlled by sound. It is this idea in the first place that set me on the path to discover this Unprecedented Elemental Reality System and inspired me to write this book. Like I explained previously, it was when I was in a yoga studio needing to explain how mantras worked when the idea of this knowledge system of the elements sprouted within me. I needed to explain how mantras, which are known as mystical or spiritual chants, can actually help us in our practical life, or, as I would say it, the physical domain. I became present not only to the fact that the subtle is more powerful than the physical and that the subtle creates the physical, but also to the fact that mantras are so powerful because they are or connect with the primordial sound, or ether element, that exists everywhere. Some people say that the original seed mantra, *om*, is "the sound of the Universe" or the core original vibrational or primordial sound that all things are made up of. This is a valid and powerful idea, but according to Vedic wisdom there is more complexity to it.

When we only look at the yoga system, which is but a small fragment of the knowledge of the Vedas, we find that each of the 72,000 energy channels, known as nadis, that exist as part of the energy or subtle body, has a unique sound. There is a yoga practice that enables the practitioner to tune into and hear the sound of each individual nadi. It is not only the nadis that have a unique sound and vibration, all things in physical reality have their own vibrational sound.

When we look at the history of the universe described in the Vedas, we find that the universe was created through the chanting of mantras by the Supreme Being, who is often called God. The Bible also supports the notion that reality was created by the divine through the medium of sound or mantra. Genesis 1:3 says, "God said, 'let there be light' and there was light."

What this all means for us is that we can have dominance over the material energy through the use of mantra or sound vibration. Certain sound frequencies can break glass or cut stone. Hospitals use sound vibration to disintegrate gallstones. If you look back at any ancient culture you can see that most have rituals that require the use of chants, mantras, music, or some kind of sound vibration. It is understood that magic systems use incantations to do their magic. This works because sound moves prana/chi/energy, and the movement of this energy moves the other physical elements.

Each bit of prana in existence has a correlative mantra or sound that can control its flow. Those who want to dominate the physical domain can learn, practice, and perfect these mantras to gain magic-like power. Perhaps the most commonly known mantras that control prana are the (bij/seed) mantras of the seven chakras (lam, ram, vam, etc.).

Again, I know this may sound woo-woo or mystical, but it is actually pretty mechanical and systematic once you understand how it all works and you have some experiences. The power of mantras was a normal part of my childhood, so I have no doubt these things work. I use them in my own life on a regular basis. Let me share two experiences from my childhood in a monastery school in India that concretely showed me the power of mantras.

There were cobras, pythons, and other types of venomous snakes in the villages of Bengal, where the monastery was located. During first aid class we were trained on what to do during different emergencies. Interestingly enough, the protocol for a cobra bite was to take the one who was bitten as fast as possible to a tantric, which is basically a shamanic villager who lives in a mud hut, to chant mantras to remove the snake poison. I have two friends who were bitten by venomous snakes and whose lives were saved by mantra chants of village tantrics. They told me that they saw the black poison enter their big toe, their toe became black, and when poked with a needle, the poison shot out—all by the power of mantra.

Another friend of mine broke his arm when he fell down a hill. He went to a similar type of tantric who fused his bone together within 24 hours simply by chanting mantras and a few other rituals. (The bad thing was that though the tantric guy had perfected the chanting of these mantras and was able to fuse the bone together, he was not a trained doctor, and the bone was not aligned properly when it was fused. My friend had to return and get his arm re-broken and refused without any anesthetic.)

I find it interesting to see how people have evolved to try to practice tantra in the Western world. The mental image I have of tantrics is of very dark and dangerous voodoo-like black magic practitioners who use dead body parts as part of their practices. In the West tantra seems to be understood as some type of sexual practice. Tantra, like yoga, is a vast, multi-faceted science that is extremely misunderstood both in the East and the West.

So mantras change the vibration of the ether element and can be used to gain dominance, control, and power over the other physical elements. Those who are sincere on the path to true enlightenment use mantra for a higher and less-selfish purpose. The second-highest use of mantra is to stabilize the mind. When we stabilize our mind we have access to a power more superior than the meagerly power of the tantrics. A stabilized mind gives us self-control, discipline, focus, and inner contentment, which are qualities that can have a much greater effect in the world than simply moving snake poison in the body. Still, mantras, being a core part of most spiritual practices and traditions, hold a higher function than simply stabilizing the mind for meditation. Mantras can be the most powerful spiritual process for connecting with the divine in passionate love. The process of such spiritual loving connection with the divine in mantra is called Kirtan and/or Japa.

Japa and Kirtan Mantra Meditation

There are many thousands of mantras, and all of them have a purpose and benefit, but not all mantras are created equal. My service to you is to give you the best, most powerful, and often-secret mantras that help both in becoming more effective in life and that will ignite true spiritual enlightenment within you, fast.

When chanting mantras there are two primary processes:

1. Japa. This is when you chant the mantra quietly to yourself. To do this is simple. Simply repeat the mantra to yourself over and over again. Try to absorb your mind fully in the mantra. Feel the sound vibration, let go of or block out any other distractions and thoughts, and simply absorb yourself in the mantras sound, feeling, and meaning.

    The effect of mantras are compounding; the longer you do them the better, so it is recommended that you start with a fixed amount of time every day, then gradually increase. You could start with four minutes then increase to 40 minutes or more. Traditionally, mantra practice is not measured in time of practice but in how many times you chant the mantra. The mediator will have a set of beads with 108 beads on it and chant the mantra on each bead, thus keeping count. They commit to a certain number of mantra iterations a day. (Go to your bonuses at *eternaldharambook.com/bonus* for links on where to get your own set of mantra meditation beads.)

2. Kirtan. This is when mantra practice is done aloud. This takes two forms. One is simply to say the mantra with more volume. This increases the "ether-ness" of the mantra practice, focuses the mind more, and helps everyone and everything that is touched by the sacred vibration of spiritual mantras. The more common practice of Kirtan is to do music and sing the mantras. This, done alone or in community, is extremely powerful. To do this, simply sing the mantras in any tune that fits and with any accompanying music. You can sing (or chant/repeat/say) mantras to yourself in the shower or while walking, driving, washing the dishes, or anywhere.

There are traditional tunes and a musical style of mantra chanting, which are not necessary but which I do love dearly.

I suggest chanting one of my favorite mantras:

Hari Bol

You can replace the mantra "Gopal" (as described in Chapter 1) with the mantra "Hari Bol" in "The Gopal Exercise Practice," or you can use this mantra (and "Gopal") for either Japa or Kirtan Meditation. Or you can just say the mantra at any volume to yourself at any time, in any place any number of times. Much benefit will still be there.

Qualities of Ether/Sky/Space/Sound: All pervading, free, open, communicative, hidden, conscious, aware, conductive, resonant, present.

Negative Qualities—when not in its healthy state: Stifled, restrained, congested.

Dharma of Ether: Ether always strives for tranquility, harmony, serenity, and peace. A good way of understanding ether is to see it as the environment. Ether wants the environment to be in a balanced equipoised state. When the environment is cluttered either with objects or obnoxious sounds, ether is disturbed.

Visual: A computer screen. Everything that goes on in your computer is shown on the same screen. The screen remains unmoved while various images move in and out of the same space on the screen.

How to Use: Ether is the midpoint between the subtle and the physical domain. Therefore it holds the power to strongly affect both domains and link them together.

1. To affect the physical domain:

You want to create tangible physical results and use sound to move air/prana energy.

1. This is commonly done in martial arts, where certain sounds are made to exert more force in a strike. Sound can also be calming. When we studied jujitsu there were certain sounds we would use when wrestling to calm the opponent and make their physical body more naturally compliant to a submission.

2. You can always use music or mantra to calm or invigorate your physical body. Calming music at night or for a massage works wonders, and upbeat music can really get your body moving and invigorate it with energy.

3. Communication is essential in creating tangible results. If a project is stuck it is possible that the ether element is also stuck; communicate and communicate some more, and things will likely get moving. Ether being the midway element between the subtle and the physical plays a key role in "translating" or "transferring" the beliefs, desires, and inspirations from the subtle domain into actual physical tangible actions and results. This translating or transferring of subtle intentions into physical results is done in two ways. One way is through communication. Though ether is sound, communication does not have to be audible to be part of the ether element. Subtle, indirect indications between like-minded individuals, visual presentations, Morse code, and so forth are all counted as ether. The other ways in which ether causes action and results in the physical domain is

through causing the movement of the air element, as previously described.

2. To affect the subtle domain:

Ether also has the ability to affect your mind/emotions, and that is often its primary use. An uncluttered tranquil and peaceful space is a requirement for anyone wanting to focus their mind. Such focus of mind and peace of emotions are essential both for the productive CEO and the reclusive mendicant spiritualist. If you are sincere on your spiritual path you must at least go through a time when you experience a complete harmony of space/ether and focus your mind on the divine in spiritual mantra meditation. Yes, it is possible and practically a crucial part of your spiritual evolution to learn to connect with the divine in peaceful meditation while acting in any situation, be it in a traffic jam, the middle of Manhattan, a war zone, or in the presence of your screaming baby. In truth the ability to do this fully takes a lifetime of practice, and a key part of such practice is to meditate in an ether-balanced environment, which is steady and supportive for focused meditation. Monastery temples are often so tranquil because such tranquility is essential in the beginning stages of meditation. Spiritual seekers often retreat from the world and go to peaceful, clutter-free places such as the Himalayan Mountains to meditate and perfect their spiritual evolution. But we on the path of Passionate Enlightenment realize that there is a higher order of being than simply retreating from the world and needing tranquility for spiritual evolution. We have much more practical and powerful processes to advance our spiritual being. Kirtan is the best process for this because it can be done in any situation and also works on the ether element. Yet still a peaceful ether-balanced situation is helpful, I recommend cleaning up your home and work space as well as going on retreats or sabbaticals.

Those looking for effective action also need a clear mind for focused attention on their work and for their creative mind to flow and discover new truths, processes, and solutions. Legendary business guru and author Peter F. Drucker said, "Follow effective action with quiet reflection, from the quiet reflection will come more effective action." This can only be done in an ether-balanced situation and with a steady mind. Many modern books have guided people how to declutter one's mind and space, so

I shall not delve into it in detail. Just know you must do it if you want to have maximum efficacy. I suggest *Getting Things Done* by David Allen and *The Life-Changing Magic of Tidying Up* by Marie Kondo.

Examples

There are many long, detailed examples I could give you for using the principle of ether/sky/sound/space in business, relationships, health, and so forth. But by now I am sure you are getting the hang of how this works and can figure out many ways of how you can use this principle. In essence, you want to make sure that there is plenty of good communication, plenty of empty space for clear thinking, and good sound vibrations such as music conducive to the state of mind you are trying to create. If you do this, any action will be supported by the principle of ether.

Ether Exercises

To increase the ether element, clean your space, go into the tranquility of nature, stay away from noise pollution (especially when working), practice the bhramari pranayama, which is a yogic berthing practice that also incorporates sound, and most importantly do mantra meditation and Kirtan.

In Medicine: Liver, gall bladder.

Chakra: 5th, throat, Visudha.

Astrology: Jupiter.

Sense Object: Sound.

Knowledge Acquiring Sense: Ears.

Mantra: Ham.

Affirmation: I tune into the harmony of space.

CHAPTER 9

THE ECHOING MIND

Congratulations! You are progressing through your training program well.

Now we will start with the subtle elements. This is the realm in which slight changes create the biggest difference. Once you learn to tune, tweak, and/or transform the subtle elements you will be unstoppable. So hold tight, my friend: The rocket is about to blast off!

People often don't think of the mind as an element. They see the mind as part of who they are, and some even believe that they *are* their mind or their intelligence. They think they *are* their thoughts and feelings and because of this they go through so much pain. The first and fundamental necessity in any spiritual path, or even any path to effectiveness, is to have some kind of accurate notion of who you are. Yes, the spiritual path is about uncovering who you really are, and igniting your fullest deepest and most beautiful potential, and that process of self-realization does take time. But still, to start on any worthwhile path you need to have at least a basic rudimentary understanding of who you are. We will explore the subject of identity in depth in Chapter 11, but for now know that just as you are not your temporary body, which will die and rot one day. You are also not your emotions, thoughts, or mind. You are something much more elegant, beautiful, and wonderful.

When we see the mind as simply another element of this mundane reality, we can begin to detach ourselves from its turmoil and experience true peace. By nature the mind is ever-changing, whereas the nature of the soul, which is you, is fixed. Therefore when we attach and identify ourselves with the constant flux of the mind we are naturally dissatisfied. The constant change of the mind is in stark contrast to the dharmic steadiness of the soul. Yes, there is place for change, transformation, and flow on the level of the soul and in the spiritual domain: True spiritual enlightenment is when you are in a constant flow and in an eternal dance with the divine. But this transcendental flow of dynamic love is of a far different nature than the restlessness and unsettledness of the mind. Thus when we understand that the mind is another element, just like earth or water, we can separate ourselves from its restless uneasiness and finally be at peace.

The Mind and Life's Dualities

This world is full of dualities: hot/cold, black/white, up/down, good/bad, happiness/distress, confidence/fear, love/hate. The mind constantly oscillates between these dualities and, if not anchored properly in a higher state of being, the mind will draw its state from these dualities, which will cause it to sometimes feel good and sometimes feel bad. Therefore, peace is impossible when the mind is out of control. Grounding the mind with spiritual practice is essential for any kind of lasting well-being. One of the main reasons meditation is repeatedly recommended by so many spiritual teachers, despite there being unlimited forms of spiritual practice, is because meditation is geared to detach the mind from the dualities of the world and center it in a higher state of being conducive for spiritual growth. When the mind is absorbed in the dualities of the world it is distracted by the happinesses and distresses of the world, and thus it becomes impossible to absorb your consciousness in the divine. A mind trapped in the saga of mundane existence cannot evolve spiritually.

What Is the Mind?

So what is the mind, anyway? In this 5,000-year-old system of the elements, the mind is distinct from intelligence. Here the mind refers specifically to the emotions or feelings. The mind is also, in a sense, your consciousness. It is also the "little voice in your head" that is always talking about what is going on and reminding you of things. The mind is the collection of thoughts in your head that happen automatically—that you are not actively focusing on. Your intelligence is the thoughts that you are deliberately choosing; intelligence comes into play when you are solving problems, creating, teaching, learning, contemplating, and so forth. The mind is all the thoughts that just run on autopilot.

Consciousness

Consciousness can have different states of being. It can vibrate at a higher or lower level and your job on the path of both Effective Action and Passionate Enlightenment is to raise the level of your consciousness, ideally to the point where you transcend above this world and enter into the spiritual domain of passionate love.

The higher the state of consciousness you have, the more effective you can be. It is like sitting on a higher platform with a better birds-eye-like view of what is actually going on. With this superior and deeper view of life, reality, and the world, you can naturally make better choices because you are not falsely absorbed in what is not real. You can see that the dualities of this world are just that: dualies, which by nature will change constantly. A simple example to illustrate this point is when someone gets angry at winter because it's cold. One of higher consciousness knows that the seasons are always changing and that summer is around the corner. Remaining steadfast in the face of the ever-changing weather and seasons is a gross example and an easier feat to accomplish than withstanding an uncontrolled mind's torment in troubling situations, such as when your lover cheats on you or leaves you, you lose your job, your business partner steals from you, or you contract a fatal disease. Social rejection is also a painful time when the mind goes bonkers and the application of true spiritual wisdom is in need. Practically applied spiritual wisdom is seen in the ability to remain equipoised, steadfast, and spiritually inspired in the face of such hardships. This does not mean to repress one's feelings, though misguided spiritual practitioners often do that in the name of spiritual advancement. It is more about raising your consciousness, ideally to a level of direct experience and relationship with God. A person of a higher level of consciousness may flow through the entire spectrum of feeling just as someone of a lower level of consciousness, but the more enlightened one will still have a superior experience with less suffering and more inner contentment.

Emotions

The world runs on emotions, and the mind is made of emotions. What we feel day in and day out is the mind element. When the mind comes in contact with the things of this world it feels something; these feelings are the mind, and they can be categorized as either positive or negative.

We often live our lives as servants of our mind; we try to seek the positive feelings we like and try to avoid the ones we don't. The search for either pleasure or liberation for suffering is what motivates most people to do almost everything they do in life. Houses are built, products are bought, people are married, wars are started, and businesses are built to support the whims of the mind. Yes, the mind is whimsical; it is always changing. What gave pleasure to the mind once loses its charm in time, and the mind searches for new sources of joy. But such sources of joy are based on the dualies of this world and cannot satisfy us. Such a life of constantly seeking for pleasure or to destroy pain is a kind of slavery, yet we are bound by the immense power of the mind, and freeing yourself from the clutches of the mind is not an easy feat.

The fastest, easiest, and most fun way to free yourself from the bondage of the mind is to use the mind to attain the divine. When we start to feel transcendental spiritual emotions, the temporary emotions of this world don't attract us as much, and our mind can flourish with the happy, joyous spiritual feelings that are constant rather than the temporary ever-changing duality-based feelings of this world. The things of this world are made of the eight elements and thus their energy and corresponding pressure is limited. The mind being the third-most-powerful element quickly sucks dry any pleasure from the eight elements and goes on a search for more. The spiritual domain, however, has unlimited potencies and thus cannot be sucked dry. There is an unlimited amount of pleasure to be had there, which is more than enough to satisfy the mind. The feelings that are a side effect of a loving God are known to be the most dharmic of emotions for the mind. Such emotions extend beyond the mind and body, and are an expression of the Eternal Dharma of the soul. The mind so beautifully aids in awakening this latent loving dharma of the soul.

I don't recommend filling your mind with spiritual emotion and thought just to pacify it, or even only to awaken your highest purpose in loving Eternal Dharma. There is immense productive power in doing so. When action is done with enough dharmic-aligned emotion, it can move mountains and is unstoppable. Take singing, for example. Someone can sing all the notes, but if they don't put the correct emotion into it the song will not move you. If a less-skilled singer sings the same or even fewer notes with ample emotion, your heart will be touched and you can be moved to action. The same principle applies to any type of action or work: When you cook with the proper love, you put more care into it and the food comes out better. When you work out and are motivated by the correct feelings, you work out harder. When you are happy you work better. When you are moved by love, you move more. This is the simple truth. We will do more and give more out of love than we will ever do for ourselves.

Just two days ago I was losing motivation in putting all the technical things together for my online course. I thought, "I was happy in the monastery and living a simple life. Why am I working so hard?" I began to introspect and came present to my mind's emotional motivation: "I am not doing this for me. This is my love offering to my Guru." This motivated me immensely and I did about four days' worth of work the next day.

I am personally working to constantly have my mind connecting with the divine in spiritual emotion because that makes me move like nothing else. Everything I do when I am feeling those feelings of spiritual love feels the best, even if it is something that is painful or tough. In the monastery I and other monks used to go begging door to door in the destitute villages of Bengal. This was our service and was done out of love. Though the sun was hot, though I even got heat stroke and other illnesses doing so, though it is embarrassing, and though people were sometimes very rude and mean, I smile in remembrance of those days. That was a burden of love, I was happy in that action, and I would do it again in a heartbeat if that was necessary in my service to my beloved Lord.

Don't be at War With the Mind

Many spiritual seekers are at war with the mind. They say it's the cause of all suffering and aim to neutralize or nullify its potency. They try to empty their head so they can exist in the peace of nothingness. Ultimately they wish the mind to die, to cease to exist, as they try to end the suffering, strife, and turmoil that the mind seems to cause. But in truth your mind, being of a more subtle and fine nature than the five physical elements, is an extremely powerful force, not to be lost. People often feel fear in the presence of power because power has the ability of immense creation or destruction. The mind is not bad, it is just the mind; it does what it does. Think of it as you think of fire not being bad: It may burn you or it may cook your food. The mind is neither friend nor foe, and the very idea of trying to stick the mind into one of these boxes is a reflection of the unhealthy relationship of the mind with the dualities of this world. Those in a higher state of consciousness do not label things as good or bad; they accept things as they are and interact with them in a way to support their spiritual growth.

People sometimes think the mind must be controlled and held back, whereas in reality the energy of the mind is best when it is enhanced, channeled, and balanced. Intelligence is the subtle element that comes before the mind in our Elemental Reality sequence, and hence intelligence must guide and focus the mind in the best direction. With the bull's-eye focus of intelligence the energy of the mind/emotions can work wonders. When I was young I learned from my elders and spiritual guides that the mind can either be your best friend or your worst enemy. Use the support of the ether element and the focus, knowledge, and clarity of intelligence to channel the energy of the mind, and you will be unstoppable in all your pursuits.

Qualities: Fast, emotional, emotive, changing, intense, inspired, moving, motivated, absorbed, present, accepting, enhancing, transparent, spontaneous, fervent, ardent, impulsive, reactive, temperamental, reflective.

Negative Qualities: Fickle, frantic, restless.

Dharma of the Mind: The mind is emotion. All feelings—the good, the bad, and the ugly—are composed of the mind element.

The mind is like a well: It is neutral and will echo out whatever sound you put into it. If you play sweet music, the well will echo it with the same amount of fervor as if you shout vulgar words into it. The immensely powerful mind absorbs itself in, and replays and repeats whatever is put into it. Have you ever had a song or a TV commercial stuck in your head, and you tried and tried to get it out but it just would not go? That is your mind echoing what was put in. Our job is to continuously feed the mind with good things, for what we put into our head is what we will get out.

Visual: A restless child that cannot sit still. This child is running from place to place and playing with everything she can find. She is happy as long as there is something to play with and what she is playing with is new fresh and shiny. She will implode and be catapulted into a dark gloom at the mere thought of sitting still, and she is elated at the sight of a new toy.

Examples of How to Use

PARTICULAR TO ELEMENT

For effectiveness in the domain of the mind detachment and neutrality are key. The mind absorbs and echoes whatever is in its vicinity and attaches meaning to it to cause emotion. This process causes turmoil and chaos, which is detrimental to effectiveness, productivity, or even sanity. When you are detached from outcomes, or from trying to feel a certain way, the process of the mind of echoing the environment and attaching meaning, which leads to emotions, is broken and you are set free. This is because the mind attaches itself most to what you are attached to you—what you desire. Therefore it's only once you detach that you can fully be at peace and in balance. When you are detached you can see things as they are without your mind influencing your perception with its subjective emotional experience, which is born from judgment. So if you want peace, cultivate neutrality and develop detachment. How to do this is a subject for another book or course, but in essence detachment can only truly happen when there is a positive attachment to the divine.

Much of the wisdom in the world, be it psychology or spiritual traditions, is aware of the negative effects of the mind. There is a lot of powerful knowledge out there on how to control the mind. Many teachers give training on how not to be affected by the chaos, and how to be present, focused, and effective. I recommend studying these things, as I myself do. The mind is an immensely powerful element that can move mountains or cause havoc, and in truth most people are slaves to their mind, so any knowledge of how to deal with this enormous force is a plus. There is nothing like the 5,000-year-old Vedic wisdom of India for channeling the energy of the mind. This is not simply because this ancient wisdom has what I understand to be the most in-depth understanding of the workings of the mind, and a plethora of practices and traditions of how to work with it, but it is also because the knowledge system does not inherently see the mind as bad. Like I mentioned before, many systems see the mind as a bad thing that must be controlled, restricted, tamed, or held back in some way, whereas the Vedic system takes quite the opposite approach. The Vedas want to increase and enhance the presence of the mind so that it can flow in full force. They want to engage the mind in the best and most positive ways, because the mind is one of the most powerful tools in both effective action and in speeding to enlightenment. The transition in the Western world from seeing the mind only with regard to disease and neurosis to positive psychology is a recent one that is only starting to take place in our lifetime, whereas the Vedic system has been doing this for at least 5,000 years and sees the goodness of the mind in the very core of its philosophy and practices. I also see that even other spiritual Eastern traditions, which focus on void, emptiness, and oneness, also come from the paradigm of seeing the mind as bad. As a friend and a guide I say to be careful and watch out for them! Any knowledge system that at its core says there is something inherently wrong with you, nature, or any of the elements, will lead to stifling you and making you feel guilty. Such self-condemning paradigms are plentiful in the spiritual and religious space, so be careful. God created all things perfectly, and to love and respect all things—be it emotion, sex, or even death—is essential if we are to love God. Don't misunderstand me here: There is beauty, power and necessity in growth, change, and personal evolution. I am an extremely passionate and driven man who constantly strives to make things better. But the key distinction is to not condemn that which needs to be evolved. A seed is perfect and beautiful, yet it still needs to grow. In the same way, the mind is what it is: It is perfect and beautiful, yet growing and evolving it is a must.

The Vedic spiritual traditions are full of dance, music, food, art, drama, feelings, mantras, physical action, information, intricate temples, exquisite art, and so much more. The reason for this is that it gives plenty of "good fuel" for the mind to get absorbed in. What you put in your mind is what you get out. So by putting good things in, your mind will naturally reflect similar things. On the spiritual path this means absorbing your consciousness in spiritual education, like reading this book, taking courses, listening to spiritual talks, mantra practice, engaging your body in spiritual rituals, Kirtan (this is the most important and powerful), cooking and offering to the divine, and so much more. The mind needs variety—that is its dharma—so give it many options and flavors to be absorbed in the divine.

For effectiveness, the process is the same: Give your mind plenty of things to get absorbed in that will specifically help with what you are trying to be effective at.

EFFECTIVE IN BUSINESS

There are so many ways you can effectively use the energy of the mind element in business, but I am writing this book in such a way as to give you the raw ingredients, so that you can find many creative ways to apply these principles yourself. Here are some key ways to use the mind for effectiveness in business.

Have spiritual emotions permeate your business culture. Emotions are motivating; that's a simple fact. The dualities of this world (good/bad, happiness/distress, etc.) affect most people's minds, and they are constantly seeking to have their mind experience the positive side of these emotions. People want the happiness and don't want the distress. Many businesses understand this and are geared to fulfill that need. They solve the problem of the negative side of the duality and/or provide the positive. This works and keeps many businesses afloat. But this is only using the principle of the mind element in its lowest form. To get the most from the principle of the mind element we need to focus on two areas: employees (or partners) and the higher and deeper need and aspiration of the customer.

Let's talk about your employees (or partners). You already learned that the nature of the world is that there are dualities and the mind is constantly "bouncing around" in a multitude of these dualities. When mature spiritual detachment has not been established, the mind feels these dualities and thus one's emotions are ever changing. A business may survive in a temporary relationship with a customer by interacting with the customer on the basis of only one side of the duality. You only call a plumber when you have an issue with the plumbing. When the other side of the duality occurs the relationship is over, or on hold, until the next time. Your employees are different: They are with you all the time and their mind/emotions by nature will be changing. When they are not feeling good, they will be less productive and their state of mind will affect your other employees and customers. This will also make the other employees less productive and will un-inspire the customers. The net result will not be favorable for your business. Savvy CEOs know this and try to keep their employees as happy as possible. But when the focus on happiness is simply part of the mind's play, the other side of the duality will eventually manifest and the same problem still remains. Business gurus know this, though perhaps not from this viewpoint, so they say that there has to be a higher purpose—a higher mission—to motivate employees. This is the right train of thought: A higher purpose is not only essential to keep you and your employees motivated for your business, but it is also key in any type of motivation in life. This strong purpose can come from one of five places, and not all of them are created equal. Let's break down a few of them.

Intelligence. Higher guidance can be based in information, reasoning, or understanding, and this can pacify and calm the mind temporarily. Yet it is not strong enough to control the mind consistently. Some people use the intelligence/information element to create company rules, such as codes of conduct, corporate bylaws, and so forth. These are most often operating in the domain of intelligence and therefore can only work temporarily.

Ego/identity. If employees identify with the higher mission and purpose of the company they can use their own intelligence (rather than the information you give them) to guide their mind, and thus more constantly be in the right emotional state to serve and produce.

Desire. Employees must want to be (have the identity) the kind of person that uses their intelligence to control their mind/feelings to be productive and create a good customer experience. Another way of saying this is that the employee must choose to identify with the mission of the company. The stronger the choice and more established the identity, the better they will perform.

Beyond this is *dharma.* It must be the employee's dharma to serve and fulfill the mission/dharma of the company. (This should make sense to you. But if the concept of dharma is not clear for you, please review Chapter 1 and 2. It is an essential part of your training to have an in-depth understanding of dharma.) This mandates that your company's mission is a dharmic one, and that it is in alignment with nature and the divine. If your business is not dharmic, there will be no one you can employ that will not hamper your business with the negatives of a temperamental mind.

This is not just about employees, you will also not be fulfilled in your business if it is not dharmic and you will also underperform. The question, then, is: Where does dharma come from? And the answer is: the Divine. The Supreme Being or God is, by definition, the origin of everything, including dharma. What the Supreme desires becomes dharma. Therefore to be in full dharma Spiritual Surrender is essential. By constantly surrendering to the will of the divine you will always be in perfect dharma, and thus you can set up or adapt your business to be a dharmic business. Then you can find people whose dharma it is to work in such a business, who can then choose your business's mission fully (desire) and thus use their intelligence to control and inspire their mind—to be in the right state of being to do their best work. Thus your business can and will flourish. The more you can facilitate your employees to connect with their deepest spiritual purpose, the more fulfilled, balanced, controlled, and effective they can be. (How to practically do this with fire-like clarity and earth-like groundedness is a topic for a course in and of itself: *myspiritualsuccess.com*)

Keep your emotions neutral when making critical decisions. This can be done by detaching yourself from the outcome and in a sense removing yourself from the situation. Leave your feelings, ego, and expectations out of the picture, and look at the problem or choices in a neutral, unbiased way. With your mind and emotions tamed you will make better choices. Of course this is helpful for any type of decision-making. Doing mantra meditation before decision-making can help settle your mind so you can be detached and equipoised in your decision-making.

On the Spiritual Path

One of my favorite verses in Vedic literature states that the entire purpose of every piece of advice and every guideline given in the vast body of Vedic wisdom is simply to get you to always remember God and never forget Him or Her. Everything in Veda is simply to lead you to remember the sweet loving beauty of the ever-seductive Supreme Being. The mind is the best tool for such blissful thought because it echoes whatever you put into it. It is the mind/consciousness that is in a sense doing the remembrance and is what you want to absorb in the Divine. Simply do Kirtan, mantra practice, and any other of the multitude of spiritual practices to fill your mind with sweet thoughts of the Divine, and your mind will echo them back to you and thus your life will become perfect. There is nothing sweeter than this. You may make a million dollars a day, meet the man or woman of your dreams, or create the largest company in the world, but such joys cannot satisfy your mind or soul like the enlightened thought of Lord's sweet face. Even altruistic activities do not satisfy the heart like the dharma of divine love; remembering God does.

Mind Exercises: I have already explained the best of the best mantra meditation practices Kirtan and Japa. They are the best things for the mind, but here are some more tips for the mind element:

- To increase feelings and emotions on a subject, get more detailed information (intelligence element, which comes before this one in the spectrum) on it, for information breeds emotions. For example, if you want to fall in love with a new habit such as exercising, learn all about it, think about it, read about it, surround yourself with others who exercise, put up a yoga poster, and so on. The detailed information from the intelligence element, plus the constant feeding of stimuli to the mind, will cause your mind to think about it and you will develop a liking and emotional affinity with it. The same principle is used in marketing: The more someone comes across your brand or product, the more emotionally comfortable and attached they become to it. Create a daily mantra meditation (Japa) practice.
- Feed your mind whatever you want more of. The mind will echo back to you what it takes in.
- Of course don't feed your mind things you don't want in your life, which means taking control of the media you consume. Considering you have read this much of the book, I assume that you already choose what type of things you want let enter you head. So good job! Continue with more stuff like this and avoid regular TV.
- Learn to be steady, equipoised, and detached. This is easier said than done. The classic book *The Bhagavad Gita* is all about doing this.

Extras for Mind

In Medicine: Emotional imbalances are one of the largest causes for disease according to Ayurveda and Traditional Chinese Medicine. To be physically healthy you must be emotionally healthy, because the subtle creates the physical. Therapy is a good thing, and there are many program and books that help heal emotional wounds of the past. It is important to heal any old relationships, specifically those with your parents. The Landmark Forum is helpful for healing the emotional body and so are affirmations, like those prescribed in the book *You Can Heal Your Life* by Louise Hay.

If you get into detail, each organ is connected to a specific emotion and an unbalanced excess or deficiency of that emotion will hurt the corresponding organ. Nervous butterflies in the stomach are an example of this, as are heavy breathing and crying in sadness or sweating in anger. But in essence, emotional repression causes sickness, so express yourself and share your feelings. Sharing allows emotions to move, which prevents excess pressure on a particular part of your body.

Chakra: The subtle elements don't correspond to the chakras like the five physical elements do. But all of the subtle elements are vast and "all pervading," so all the chakras are permeated by the mind element. In fact each chakra has a corresponding emotion which is the mind element.

Astrology: Moon.

Sense Object: The subtle elements don't correspond to the senses as the five physical elements do.

Knowledge Acquiring Sense: The subtle elements don't correspond to the senses as the five physical elements do.

Mantra: No specific mantra, but all mantras are good, specifically those that are meant to inspire emotions and feelings for the divine, such as the mantras prescribed in Chapter 16.

Affirmation: I love you, my Lord.

CHAPTER 10

THE CALCULATIONS OF INTELLIGENCE

Ah, intelligence—what a beautiful element. Intelligence has the power to create anything and make any experience, no matter how hurtful, be painless. You are going to like this one, my friend.

In our head there are several "voices" or perspectives from which we see and interact with reality. So far, of these "voices," we have discussed the mind, but there is also the intelligence, the ego, and desire. Plus whether we hear it or not, there is the voice of divine guidance always pulsating in our heart. Some people call this intuition, but I see it as God, the all-pervasive seer of all things, talking to you. Differentiating between each of these "voices" is extremely valuable especially when we are dealing with the main subjects of this book: Effective Action and Passionate Enlightenment. As you study this book, you learn and gradually develop the skill to differentiate the "voices." It takes practice, but because you have read this far, I think you will get it and become really good at it.

Know that, out of all the things that go on in your head and heart, it is your intelligence that does the understanding, comprehending, and analyzing.

Intelligence vs. Mind

When the mind comes in contact with any element, which basically means when it interacts with anything of this world, it automatically reacts, echoes, and feels emotions. Which emotions are felt is based on the previous experiences of the mind, because the mind simply reflects or echoes back what has been put in. The intelligence, on the other hand, does not react to the elements with feeling but understands them instead. It is the intelligence that sees things as they are and understands the "hidden" truth of things.

> ### Example
>
> Let's say you are walking at night and see a long, curvy thing on the ground. When your mind comes in contact with it, it will immediately react based on your previous experiences. If you have lived in a place where there are snakes or have just been watching movies involving snakes, the mind may think it's a snake and get scared. When the intelligence kicks in, it will deliberate to see what the real truth is. It may say, "I am in New York City. There are no snakes here, and—look—it's not moving, I can see its tassels. It's not a snake, it's a rope."

When differentiating the mind from the intelligence, remember it is the mind that reacts, echoes, and feels; and it is the intelligence that understands, comprehends, and analyzes.

Intelligence comes before the mind in the Elemental Spectrum. Therefore it controls the mind. When the intelligence sees things as they are, it relaxes or excites the mind, and the mind will react emotionally to the information provided by the intelligence. The intelligence says "red car" and the mind says "yay!" The intelligence says "enemy" and the mind say "grrr."

The sad truth is that most people live through their mind rather than through their intelligence, and therefore suffer excessively and are blind to the truth. The duty or dharma of intelligence is to know the truth, and most people care more about what feels good than what the truth is. They say ignorance is bliss. And such choice of mind or good feelings over thinking and learning the truth is what keeps people in pain, unsuccessful, and ineffective. If you want to live a powerful life, choose intelligence over emotion and constantly strive to go deeper into the truth. By doing this you can control your mind and be informed in the choices you make. The more informed you are, the more information you will have in decision-making. The more information you have in decision-making the better decisions you can make and better decisions lead to a better life.

Layers of Truth

Oscar Wilde said, "The pure and simple truth is rarely pure and never simple." He was right in understanding that the truth is not simple. Truth comes in layers, and the more you dig into it, the more detail and dimension you will find. You can constantly dig deeper and deeper into truth and find more and more dimensions and details in it. Take something as simple as a rock, for example. The first-layer truth is it's just a rock, pure and simple. When you look deeper, it is sedimentary rock, which is made up of sand, shells, pebbles, and other fragments of material. When you look deeper, each grain of sand is made up of different minerals and other substances, and deeper than that of atoms. Deeper than the atoms are protons, neutrons, and electrons, which make an atom. And on an even deeper level, protons and neutrons are made of quarks. Then the questions come: What are quarks? What is a neutron and a proton? What types of minerals make up the grain of sand? Why and how did the sand come together to form a rock? What is the rock being used for? What shape is it? What's its temperature? And so on.

There is more of the intelligence element than any other element excluding ego/identity. So there is infinite knowledge to be learned.

Then the question that comes up is how much to learn. Some people get so intellectual and into understanding things that they can be cold and annoying to be around, and such overthinking can stop them from being able to be effective and happy. An excess of knowledge can be a bad thing, just as a deficiency of knowledge is. This is true for all the elements, and imbalance of any element is what causes disease. Too much fire in your house will burn it; too little fire will freeze it. There needs to be the correct amount in proportion to the other elements for a dharmic and happy optimal state. Intelligence needs to be balanced with emotion/mind and identity. Too much thought without feeling makes you hard-hearted. But too much feeling without thought is ignorance. So back to the same question: How much thought and intelligence are needed in any given situation? The answer is enough to bring a clear understanding of your direction and next actions, so that you can make an informed choice and be practically effective, and not too much that it makes you cold and hard-hearted. Plus you don't want to fall into the trap of paralysis of analysis.

I must say, though, that relying on your intelligence for managing happiness and being effective works to a certain extent, but it cannot satisfy the deeper you. A higher form of guidance is essential for true effectiveness and happiness.

Quick Tip 1: If you are in pain because of any situation, learn more about the inner truths of what is going on and learn more about the nature of life, reality, and the spiritual path. The light of proper knowledge destroys the suffering of the mind.

Quick Tip 2: If you want a higher quality of life make better choices. Make better choices by learning and knowing more. Dig deeper into the truth of the situation and subjects at hand, there is always more to know.

Quick Tip 3: If you are overwhelmed with too much of the information/intelligence element from following Quick Tip 2, and thus can't make a good choice, decrease this intelligence element by increasing the element after it on the spectrum (mind/emotion). This is a fancy Elemental Reality way of saying "follow your heart." Bring tenderness, feelings, emotions, and sensitivity into the mix, and this will soften the hard and cold analytical-ness of intelligence. The "follow your heart" advice is poison when there is insufficient intelligence in the mix, and it is nectar when there is excess information or the intelligence element. Thus in everything, balance is key.

The Spiritual Path

The spiritual path is all about connecting with the divine in passionate love, and this connection is above the elements. It happens on the level of the soul and thus is independent from intelligence. Yet still our intelligence is a powerful tool on our spiritual journey.

Just like medicine, spiritual practices work whether you understand them or not. But by understanding how and why they work, and what they will do for you, your intelligence is satisfied and will not oppose your practices. If the intelligence understands the sense in what you are doing, it will turn into your ally and support, encourage, and even outright force you to do whatever you need to do, such as spiritual practice. This is why I teach spiritual knowledge: I want your intelligence to support you on your spiritual journey. In actuality, you only need a strong desire and a heart full of love to advance on the spiritual path; intelligence is not required. Just like people who have physical health problems due to an imbalance of the five physical elements, there are plenty of intellectually challenged people who are moving closer to God: He, She, or however you define It does not discriminate. Love is love, and God likes that. Yet still, being healthy and highly intelligent is helpful on the spiritual path, therefore I also I share with you how to be healthy and smart. Discipline is required for any type of success, spiritual or worldly; and proper knowledge, be it reasons why or knowledge of how it all works, is necessary for the intelligence to promote such discipline. Therefore knowledge is king, and I always keep learning, my friend.

Spiritual life is an offering of loving service. When we are fully enlightened we do that service with only our soul. We love and serve with the inner chambers of our heart, which is beyond the elements of this world. But in order to reach that state of full Passionate Enlightenment we must use the elements in service. In the religious space people will use elements such as earth and water to build temples or churches or to do ritual offerings. This is good. By engaging the elements in service, we spiritualize them and such actions help us advance. The intelligence is the second most subtle and thus the second most valuable, powerful, and important element, and therefore must be an extremely powerful tool to use in spiritual service. I remember having my heart touched when I read in the Bhagavad-Gita that simply by reading, hearing, or learning the philosophy of the Divine we are serving the Divine with our intelligence. The process of spiritual education is a spiritual process in and of itself. Therefore simply by reading this book, especially the later chapters that are more spiritually focused, you are advancing on the loving path of enlightenment. I am so grateful to be a part of it.

Intelligence: The Creative Tool

Because intelligence analyzes and comprehends things, it has a database of information about various things. When the intelligence is functioning well, it does not just store this data, but it also mixes it together to make "new" things. This is creativity. It may seem that when we are creative we are making new things, but the truth is we are just mixing old things in a new way.

This Elemental Reality System is my creation—no one has presented a system like this before—yet it is not new. I have compiled and combined information from various sources and am simply presenting ancient wisdom in a new way. This is how all creation works. That's why

Albert Einstein said, "The secret of creativity is knowing how to hide your sources."

The motor car, as an example, was a new invention when it was created, but seats, wheels, engines, doors, and the concept of travel were not. Mr. Ford just put old ideas together in a new compilation. This is what intelligence does. We do it every day in many areas of our life, such as in our cooking and eating. Even though thinking and creativity are natural for a healthy, elementally balanced human being, most people are not balanced and therefore are ineffective and unfulfilled. This is probably why Henry Ford said, "Thinking is the hardest work there is, which is probably the reason why so few engage in it."

It is important to know that the real creator is the Divine; all things come from that supreme and exquisitely beautiful being. The Supreme Divine Being creates all things with a built-in dharma. Instead of trying to artificially take the role of God, we are best served by finding dharma and acting in accordance with it. There is more power in this approach. Some people may think that this is stifling, but it's not; it is freeing and empowering. The best music comes when the musicians surrender to the natural flow of the music; they have tuned into dharma of the song, and that is when magic is made.

Contemplation: Think of something you may have invented or came up with. Then think to find what the sources were of your idea. What inspired those ideas? What other ideas did you draw from to come up with your creations?

Quick Tip: To be creative, try to have many experiences in life and learn many different genres of knowledge. This way you will have a large body of knowledge for your intelligence to draw from and create with.

Non-Conscious Intelligence

Intelligence, being the second most subtle element, just like ether, is present everywhere. When I was contemplating this element, its esoteric spiritual side came to mind. Just as the divine is all-pervading, so is His or Her consciousness and intelligence. I saw how this understanding is useful for connecting with and tuning into the will of the Divine, but I knew that, just like all Vedic concepts, there must also be a less-spiritual side to this concept of all pervading intelligence that is helpful for those who have not yet experienced a connection with the Divine, or who are not convinced that such a Supreme Being exists. And it clicked.

The intelligence element does not just exist as the cerebral side of living conscious beings. Intelligence is also math, data, and information. In computer science the 1s and 0s that software programs are made from are the intelligence element. The human intelligence that is used to comprehend these principles and to program the 1s and 0s is also intelligence, and so is the order in which the 1s and 0s stand after the human is gone.

The physical elements exist under the auspicious of the subtle ones, and every object is a composition of all eight elements. As I write this I am looking at a pencil on my desk and thinking, "Where is its intelligence?" It surely has no brain and no consciousness, mind, intelligence, or ego of its own. It has no desires and is simply inert matter. Yet the intelligence element is there. An inventor invented it, and its shape was intelligently designed for a reason (to fit in your hand when you write). Now this pencil sits on my desk with the same shape and specifications born from intelligence. Without this intelligence the pencil would be a pile of led and wood, and with intelligence it is a pencil. Intelligence exists in the pencil just like any other element. It is just subtle and requires intelligence to see and perceive it.

The words on this page are the intelligence element, the actual ink is predominantly water and earth, but the organization of that ink into letters that communicate information and ideas was done by intelligence and therefore is the intelligence element. As an author I have encoded my intelligence into these pages, yet when you read my book I am not there;

you only have the intelligence existing in the order of the words. From this we can see that the intelligence element, though dependent on consciousness, can also exist as unconscious matter.

But some people would argue that, by reading someone's work or by watching videos of them, a connection and relationship is created. They would say that it's cold to say that there is no actual love in a love letter. I feel like I know many authors simply by reading their work and I feel like I know people from watching their YouTube channels. In our time together through this book, I am trying to create a relationship with you, so there is one part of me that agrees that it is not possible to completely divorce intelligence from the intelligent. Where there is information there is consciousness.

This Elemental Reality System also agrees by saying that inert physical matter is made up of the first five and the three subtle elements are indeed an expression of and connected to consciousness and life. The implications of the three subtle elements being inseparable from consciousness are vast. DNA and mathematical laws are the intelligence element, so the knowledge of the inseparability of intelligence from the intelligent would also support the vastly popular notion that there is a greater consciousness in the Universe that is beyond human intelligence. Some would call this consciousness The Universe and others would call it God; I have been referring to it as the Divine. The 5,000-year-old wisdom of Veda therefore says that to understand the elements and physical reality we must also study this greater consciousness. We must also know the Universe and we must know "God." This Elemental Reality System will work powerfully without knowing the Divine. If you are an agnostic or atheist, I understand; there is a lot to figure out in the world, and who can really say if God exists, especially without directly experiencing Him? Oftentimes religions and spiritual people don't have the life or maturity that would inspire anyone to believe what they say. So I understand and do not care to change anyone's beliefs. As part of my duty in teaching this Elemental Reality System, I must say that it is infinitely more powerful and effective when you have the love, support, and guidance of the greater power that created it all.

Qualities: Knowledge, creativity, understanding, cerebral acumen, rational, logic, reason, data, and information.

Negative Qualities: Boring, emotionless, dry.

Dharma of Intelligence: Strives for truth. Wants clarity, definition, understanding, knowledge, and information.

Visual: An encyclopedia full of lists and chapters containing information on everything and anything.

Excess: Paralysis of analysis. Fun is destroyed. Increases God Syndrome. We can never know it all, but excess intelligence may make you think you can and you can be blind to the good advice of others and the guidance of the Divine. Waste time striving for useless knowledge.

Deficiency: Bad choices, minimizes power in all other elements, confused, dull.

How to Tweak: Increased by ego/identity. Decreased by mind/emotions.

Intelligence Activities: Reading, writing, introspecting, learning, math, debating, and analyzing.

How to Use: Use the intelligence to get clarity and to obliterate confusion. Create with intelligence. Tame the mind with intelligence. Have all of your actions founded in a strong base of this subtle element and this will increase your effectiveness many-fold. This may seem like a given, but in this world it is the most lacking element of them all. Think before you act.

Examples

Intelligence for Pain Destruction: Life sometimes sucks, and we think that is what causes us to suffer. But in actuality suffering is simply an experience that takes place in the mind/emotions element. The same crisis could happen to two different people, or even to the same person at a different time, and one may suffer while the other does not. This is because, in one sense, suffering is simply the judgment and experience of the mind. Therefore, when the emotions/mind are in steadiness and balance, and are situated correctly, suffering is minimized or even eradicated. This fact is one of the reasons why people become happier when they start meditating. Meditation and the use of the ether element in mantra, and music will restrain hold and harmonize the mind and thus bring it peace and tranquility. But, my friends, there is another essential lever to balance the mind—the element from which the mind was born and which it depends on, the element before it in the Elemental Spectrum: Intelligence. Emotions can only be derived from information. For example, you can only feel the pain of your mother's death if you know she has died and you can only feel the pain of a cut on your leg if your nerves deliver the information of the cut to your brain. Knowledge alone can cause the pain of a cut to increase. Have you ever had a cut or injury that did not hurt much until you saw how bad it was? It is the intelligence element in the form of information that allows suffering to exist. Therefore correcting information has the power to eradicate suffering. If you are mourning the death of your mother and you find out that she is alive, the suffering you were going through will diminish and disappear. The ancient knowledge of Veda stresses the importance of continuous education of life, the world, and the Divine in order to diminish the various pains of life. The more we are situated in true knowledge the less we suffer.

The Story of the Prince and the Saint

Once upon a time in ancient India there was a prince who had a close minister friend. This minister was well versed in the Vedic knowledge and was very spiritually evolved.

One day this young prince approached his minister and was sad. He was crying because his fastest and favorite horse had escaped and ran to the forest. Upon hearing this, the minister began to smile and laugh. The prince knew the minister was not the envious type and could not understand how his friend was happy in a time when he was supposed to be sharing his grief.

After some time the horse returned with a herd of wild horses, and thus the stable of the prince tripled in size. The prince was elated and told his minister that now he understood why the minister was happy. The horse leaving was not a bad thing; it was a good thing.

Some days later the prince was riding one of the new horses and the untrained wild horse bucked, causing the prince to fall to the floor and break a leg. When the minister visited the injured prince he was very happy. Again the prince was crying and the enlightened minister was laughing. The prince could not understand how his close friend could be so heartless. How could his minister, who was so near and dear and who always had his best interest in mind, be happy at his injury? So the young prince had the minister arrested and jailed. The enlightenment minister was smiling and happy all the while, which puzzled the prince even more. Why was this highly intelligent minister always happy at the wrong times? He seemed to have it backward.

In time the prince healed and went on a trip to the forest. The prince was captured by tribal savages and was soon to be killed and offered as a human sacrifice to the Goddess of the tribesmen. Just before the ceremonial murder, the head priest noticed an imperfection in the offering: The prince's leg was damaged and according to their ritual standards, they were unable to offer an imperfect injured human in sacrifice. They let the prince go.

Being thankful for his life the prince realized that his close friend the minister knew that things are not always as they seem. What seems like a blessing can be a curse, and what seems like a curse may be a blessing.

He returned, released his minister from prison, and began to inquire from his minster about the nature of life, reality, and what is good and bad. He said that he understood how the minister saw the blessing hidden in his apparent misfortunes of losing his horse and breaking his leg, and how the minister saw the misfortune in the apparent fortune of the horse returning with many others. The prince inquired to his wise minister why the minister had to undergo so much trouble in jail. The minister replied that if he was not jailed he would have accompanied the prince to the forest, and when captured the tribesmen would have found him to be a worthy offering.

What seems good may be bad and what seems bad may be good. Therefore those who are wise do not absorb their consciousness in judging good and bad and rather use their intelligence to fix their mind on what will really benefit them on the deepest level: transcendental loving spiritual consciousness. When one is highly intelligent, they naturally become detached to the apparent dualities of the good and bad of this world, because they know that things are not what they seem. And thus the suffering of the mind is nipped at the bud.

Introspection

Think back into your life and find a pain or tribulation you went through that was not fun at the time but that helped you grow to be the better person you are today. How would your life be now if you had not gone through that trial? What essential qualities would you be missing in yourself if you had not gone through the pain?

CHAPTER 11

THE HIDDEN POWER OF IDENTITY

The Hidden Power of Identity, according to the wisdom of the ancients, your sense of self, your belief in who are you are, and what I call your ego or identity, is simply another element in the Elemental Spectrum. It is just as malleable as, or perhaps even more malleable than, any of the other elements, and it is something you can, and must, adjust to in order to be maximally effective or to truly ascend on the spiritual path of Passionate Enlightenment.

What Is Ego/Identity?

The ego/identity is the element of self-belief. It is the element that thinks you are who you think you are. Ego/identity is the element that says what type of person you are, and is your values and beliefs. What you believe you are good and bad at, and how you perceive yourself is all ego/identity. Confidence and self-esteem (and the lack thereof) exist in this element, and it is this element that makes the intelligence think, "This is who I am and therefore this is what I do." The "who I am" part of the last sentence is the ego/identity speaking.

You and Your Ego/Identity

Because of the nature of ego/identity, it's important to note that you may not be who you think you are. You are the soul, which is pure by nature; you are a consciousness that is beyond your temporary and ever-changing body and mind. In actuality you are not made of any of the elements, yet they cover you in the form of both the physical (earth, water, fire, air, ether) and subtle (mind, intelligence, ego/identity) bodies.

In order for you to be able to function with these two elemental bodies that cover you, the extremely subtle and fine element of false ego or identity is the first element that covers you, the soul. It is the ego/identity element that has you think that your hand is you, whereas in actuality it is simply a sophisticated clump of skin, bone, blood, and nerves. It is the ego/identity element that, in a sense, bewilders you and makes you think you are your subtle and physical bodies.

The more subtle the element, the greater volume of it exists, and therefore there is plenty of ego in the world. You and I have a multitude of identities, and these identities are what drive us to think, feel, and act in whatever way we do. You may understand why this is by now: The ego/identity element leads to the intelligence element, which leads to the mind/emotions, which lead to action in the physical domain or the five elements. (I explain this in detail in the next chapter.) Therefore every action we take and every thought of our intelligence is rooted in a certain identity, and we all have a multitude of identities. We can identify as a parent, a member of a certain race, by our job, and by our skills all at the same time, for example.

The more obvious part of the identity element is seen when we think we are a certain race, nationality, color, gender, age, height, weight, and so forth. But there are many other forms of identity that are less obvious but are extremely key in shaping our lives. Competencies, such as being a good painter, singer, business person, sportsman, or knitter, are a good example of this. If we believe we are capable of something then our intelligence will find or create the knowledge needed to accomplish what we believe we are good at. At the same time, if we don't believe we are capable, we will sabotage ourselves so that reality remains in alignment with our ego/identities idea of reality.

In a way you can say that ego/identity element is where our understanding of reality lies, and because it is so subtle and so powerful, it forces the intelligence, mind, and other elements to create a reality that is in alignment with what it believes. That's why Henry Ford said, "Whether you think you can or you think you can't, you're right." Here are some examples of what I mean.

Positive Example

My beneficial temporary dharma is as teacher and guide. I use my dharma in the best way I can by teaching this immaculate wisdom and helping people be effective while reaching enlightenment. But occasionally I coach some people in other areas that I am good at, such as yoga, exercise, or martial arts. When doing this I often have a student who does not believe that they are strong enough to do a certain exercise, or flexible enough to do a certain yoga pose. As a teacher who can tell where the student is, I can see that their physical body is capable and it is only their self-image (ego/identity) that is stopping them. At this point showing them how to do the exercise or yoga pose over and over again is useless. What I do instead is re-align their ego/identity with the reality that they can do the pose. One way I do this is by physically putting their body in the yoga pose. When they see that they actually can do it, their ego/identity changes and they can then do it on their own.

Another example would be of someone who is less physically able to do the pose, but because of such strong belief in their self, ego/identity element, they find a way and quickly excel.

Negative Example

Since childhood I had the self-belief that I am a terrible artist; I can't draw, and my handwriting is messy. My teacher made me spend lots of time practicing my handwriting, so I actually have good skill and technique, but my identity does not accept it. Sometimes I will be in the middle of writing something or drawing a diagram and it will be neat or even quite good, and my ego can't take it. The ego can't stand seeing reality as different from its identity. I immediately have to sabotage it. I have notebooks full of sentences that are neat in the beginning and messy at the end.

———

It is important that you have an understanding of your identities; here are some examples of different identities so that you can get a better idea of what I am talking about: mother, father, husband, wife, child, mature, capable, good cook, strong, weak, intelligent, slow, good carpenter, computer whiz, loser, spiritual, motivated, dominant, author, teacher, inspiration, dangerous, sexy, funny, messy, clean, reserved, introvert, extrovert, genius, yoga girl, normal, fat, pretty, ugly, handsome, outsider, good/bad speaker, good/bad hockey player, logical, Christian/Muslim/Jewish/Hindu, rich, poor, healthy, health-food eater, not a health-food eater, dog lover, cat person, hat enthusiast, movie lover, artist, musician—and the list can go on and on and on. There is more of the ego/identity element than any other element.

Identifying Identity Exercise

Doing this exercise will prepare you for the other exercises coming up in this chapter.

1. Write down a list of some of your identities. Who do you see yourself as?

2. Next to each identity write five thoughts or actions it causes you to perform. The idea of this is to get you thinking deeply about how much the identities you have affect your thoughts and actions. The number (five) is only to get you thinking, but an established identity will lead you

to hundreds, thousands, or even millions of thoughts and actions. Example:

Identity: Father

Actions: 1. Care for my children. 2. Control my impulses and emotions so I can be a role model. 3. Work my job/ run my business. 4. Tell Dad jokes. 5. Scare my daughter's boyfriends.

Identity: Know-it-all

Actions: 1. Put extra energy into understanding things others don't. 2. Raise your hand to answer questions in class. 3. Start explaining things to people whenever the opportunity arises. 4. Either go to learn more, or not go, because you believe you already know. 5. Become a teacher for your career.

Identities Change

When the ego/identity element is strong, it is hard for us to see that this is just an identity that we have taken on and it is not really us. We just see it as who we are, often without question. We think, "I am the strong/ funny/sexy/old/young one and that's just me." But the truth is we were not always that way, and we will change.

Mothers often have an identity crisis when their children leave home. Obviously they did not have the identity of being a mother when they were young, but after 18 years or more it is often hard to imagine being someone or something else. It almost feels like it was always that way, and when their kids leave they are lost.

This same type of unhealthy ego/identity is seen everywhere. Those who think they were strong were not strong as babies. Fat people were not fat when they were in the womb, nor were tall people tall. Identities are taken on for some time and then they are gone; this is the nature of life. When you become a parent or get married a new identity is created and in time that identity is solidified, and just as it was created it must end one day either by a life change, death, or choice.

Quick Tip

The beauty of knowing that identity is just another element that is changeable and not really us, is that now we
don't suffer too much with the the "Who am I?" dilemma
and "mid-life crises."

Don't get me wrong here: It is of highest importance to
know who you really are, and one of the main purposes
of this book is help you realize that, but who you are is
spiritual and beyond the elements, and by knowing this
you can be less stressed about choosing your temporary
identities of this life. Having said that, choosing those
identities is also key, but they are secondary—and knowing this frees us from some of the mental stress and suffering caused such existential crises.

Observing Your Identity for Power

When we become aware that the subtle creates the physical and that identity is the most subtle element, we can start to have fun in observing our
current identities and witness how these self-conceptions are what dictate
our realities, experiences, and results.

We already know that we can tweak and adjust the elements. We also
know that our identity is adjustable. With this knowledge we can then
adjust our identities to be the best ones to create the exact results we
want in life. This is one of the most powerful keys to any type of power
or success.

Choosing Your Identities

The question then arises as to which identities we should take on. There
are two factors in this:

1. Desire. This is the first and foremost factor. Desire is not a
   material element. Desire is part of the soul—part of the core

you. Your desires, though they influence when you are identifying with your two bodies, do not come from anywhere else; they are truly you. You are your desires. So take on the identity of who you want to be. You need desire to fuel your identity anyway, because it is the next thing on our elemental spectrum.

2. Dharma. The closer you align your identities with your two dharmas (Beneficial Temporary Dharma and Eternal Dharma; see Chapter 3) the more powerful they can be. If your identities are in alignment with you dharmas, you will need to put less energy into maintaining them and they will satisfy you more.

Another way of saying this is to pick your goals and choose which identities to take on based on your goals. Your identity will breed the intelligence needed to execute them.

Quick Tip

Find and eliminate any ego/identities that are harmful or unsupportive of your goals.

Creating Identity Exercise

Completing the first exercise in this chapter "Identifying Identity" should have shown you how much your identities affect your life. Therefore I recommend consciously choosing your identities.

1. Make a list of your goals, or take out your list of goals from wherever you store them.
2. Find your identities that pertain to this goal and write them down. Write down both the supportive and unsupportive ones. I guarantee you that the goals that you are not achieving will either have an unhealthy identity around it and/or a lack of the type of identity needed to accomplish it.

3. Single out the ego/identities that don't serve you and obliterate them. Obliterate them by increasing the intelligence element around them. Find and write down all the evidence that shows the identity not to be true. And every time that self-conception surfaces, use your desire and your intelligence to not let it in your head. Intelligently analyze and debate if the identity has no more hold on you. Use the evidence you wrote down as ammunition in obliterating the unwanted identity. It will lose its teeth and leave you alone.

4. Select the identity or identities that you do want.

5. Increase your desire for being that person. I am tempted to give you a trick on how to do this, but any trick will be less effective. You simply need to tap into yourself more and connect more with your core desire for the power of your desires to increase and become clear. Connect with your inner and higher self to thus connect with your desire to create or increase this new identity. If you are having trouble doing this, you may need to quiet the noise of the elements of this world, and enter into a zone where your consciousness is just filled with you and nothing else. Do the meditation described in a previous chapter to get in this zone, then just be in a quiet place and connect with your inner desire. If by doing this you still don't find strength, it means that your desire is not strong (you don't really want it), so I suggest you select a different identity or goal that is what you actually want. Other people and society can influence us to aspire for a certain goal or identity, and when we are influenced by them our desire remains weak, because the real power of desire can only come from you. You want what you want and no one can make you want something else.

6. After you have intensified your desire to have a certain identity, use the rest of the physical elements to support your new identity.

Intelligence

- Find evidence to support your identity.
- Learn what someone with that self-image would learn or know.
- Depending on the significance of the identity you are creating, you can change your name or add a title. Here are some examples: The queen knighting someone and adding "Sir' to their name; institutions awarding titles such Dr., PhD, General, CEO, and so forth. When you have a child your identity changes and now you are now a dad or a father. A woman often changes her last name when she gets married. You don't have to wait for an institution or society to change your name. Best-selling author Harv Eker changed his name to T. Harv Eker. The T stands for "The." I have heard this was to increase his identity as unique and valuable in the world. I give people personal, quirky, relationship-based nickname titles to cultivate specific identities in them. You can also create not-so-public names or phrases for yourself that solidify the identity you are creating.

Mind

- Set up the other things in your life so that your mind echoes back the feelings and identities that you want. For example, if you want to be an actor, go to actors' events. Even if you are not one yet, you will start to feel like one.
- Create emotions that help you feel like the person you want to be. Affirmations, The Secret, and many other things in popular self-help resources teach you to do this.

5 Physical Elements

Yes, the subtle creates the physical, but the physical affects the subtle. To create emotions in the mind element and to create an identity, set up physical things to remind and reinforce the identity and feelings you are creating. Wedding rings, crowns, and uniforms are good examples of this. How you dress has a huge impact on identity. It not only affects how you perceive yourself but also how others perceive you. You want others to perceive you in a way that enhances the identity you are choosing because social expectation has the largest impact on identity. There are so many ways to use the physical to inspire a subtle feeling or belief, so get creative. If you want to be an artist, leave cans of paint and paint brushes around your room. If you are getting into business, wear a business suit. Hang nunchucks if you are getting into martial arts. I have certain things hanging on my wall that have meaning for me and reinforce identities that I am creating.

Rituals and Ceremonies

Every culture that I know of has rituals and ceremonies that solidify identities. Whether it is the tribal rites of passage for a young man, wedding or the inauguration of a building, a new identity is being created. These rituals generally include special dress, sound vibrations, symbolic physicality, and social affirmation. God, being the source of all the elements, is also generally invoked in such rituals. In the Vedic spiritual tradition I come from there are elaborate ceremonies to initiate one into the spiritual path. A new name is given to the initiate, and a new dress, prayer beads, and other physical items are all given. New social roles and privileges are also assigned in such ceremonies. All of this is to support and establish a new identity. Find existing rituals to establish your chosen identity, whether it's becoming a black belt, getting a certification, or finding a spiritual Guru.

The Sanskrit word for ego/identity in the Wedic literature is *ahankara*. Ahankara is a combination of two words: *aham*, which means "I"; and *kara*, which means "do." So the name for this element literally means "I am the doer." Therefore the element is a declaration of confidence. On the positive side, a strong amount of this element has you believe that you can do whatever your ego/identity says you can, and therefore you can and will do more and be more powerful. One of our gurus would translate ahankara as "false ego," because in truth, we don't do anything; the natural flow of nature does everything according to the will of the divine.

On the Spiritual Path

The ancient spiritual wisdom of the East tells us that just as identity can be empowering, it can also cause bondage. If you want to truly advance spiritually, it is key to have the ego/identity element be in as much alignment with your Eternal Dharma as possible. This means to see yourself as and believe yourself to be first and foremost a servant of the Divine—a lover of God.

When we identify more and more with our core spiritual nature, our Eternal Dharma, then every action we take, with our physical and subtle bodies, will be aimed at executing our dharma. Thus we speedily advance in our spiritual growth.

My dear friend, this wisdom of the elements can be used for winning wars, it can be used to make multi-national corporations, and it can be used to seduce, but its highest and best application is when it is used in love—not just any love that dies when both lovers' bodies decompose in the grave, but a love that is beyond the body, one that is beyond the mind, the intelligence and ego, the passionate-blissful-loving union of the individual soul and the Divine.

(Not So) Quick Tip

To use the identity element in spiritual growth, one of my favorite gurus in history outlines six beliefs or identities to take on. Once you take on these six egos/identities, your spiritual path will enter a new phase, and you will evolve and advance in spiritual love with such high speed and compounding velocity that your entire life will change and you will easily and regularly enter into new realms of ever increasing spiritual joy. This is not cheap; it is a lifetime of practice, but you can do it.

If you become a person who takes on the following six identities, I will worship you with the core of my being, for the spiritual domain will be yours.

Here they are:

1. I only accept those things in my life that will help me advance in my connection with the Divine.

2. I reject those things that are unfavorable that take me away from my spiritual journey.

3. My protection comes from the Divine. I know the Divine is ultimately in control of everything in the Universe, His or Her power is by definitions the greatest, and due to my relationship, I am safe.

4. The Divine is my only maintainer. I know that everything on Earth and beyond is supported and nourished by the Divine. Planets revolve on their axis, plants grow, and the sun rises every morning. All of this is done by the will of the Supreme, so He or She will have no issue in supporting me.

5. I surrender fully to the Divine. I know that in the trust of love our relationship will deepen. I let the Divine guide me in everything I do.

6. I choose to imbibe humility. Great egos are always smashed; I choose confidence, yet I am not deluded with a sense of false power. A place of humble servitude to the Divine is an exquisitely fun and beautiful one, it ironically awards great power, but I don't do it for that. I do it for love.

I know these identities are difficult to take on, especially when we are steeped in a strong sense of God Syndrome, where we want to enjoy and dominate and lord over nature. But at least we can aspire to take on one or two of these identities at a time and gradually increase, for the sweetness of loving surrender is the best.

Qualities: Hidden but more present than any other element, defining, influencing, inspired, inherent, confident, competent.

Negative Qualities: Proud, arrogant, egotistical, deluded.

Dharma of Ego/Identity: The duty of the ego/identity element is to provide direction for the rest of the elements. The intelligence and mind don't know what to think if they don't know who they are. You can see this problem with people who are lacking in this element: They feel lost and don't know what to think or feel and are therefore ineffective in life.

Visual: A confident leader king or CEO, walking into a room of subordinates. Simply by his presence everyone begins to move and do what they are supposed to be doing. If there is any doubt of what is right or should be done, the king can give direction with minimal effort and all else follows.

When to increase: Increase the ego/identity element when you want to accomplish something or you need an extra boost in a project or solving a problem.

Excess of Ego/Identity Element: If you have too much of it you can be over-confident, and thus lack the humility needed to put in the actual work and due diligence.

Deficiency of Ego/Identity Element: Makes one lethargic, unmotivated, confused about what to do with life, purposeless, and waste talent or potential.

How to Increase: Desire, though not an element, comes before ego/identity in my elemental spectrum, and therefore is needed to increase the element. If there is a will, there is a way; strong desire is everything. Intelligence, though it tampers ego, is also a useful tool in supporting a healthy identity. Earth supports water and air supports sound/ether, in the same way intelligence supports identity. That means find evidence and information to support your self-image.

How to Decrease: Intelligence decreases ego. When you think you are all that powerful and when you think you are all that, it only takes the intelligence to look at the facts and find that really you are dependent on others, dependent on nature, and dependent on God. In actuality you are completely dependent and insignificant in the grand scale of the millions and millions of galaxies in the Universe.

Identity-Enhancing Activities: Any social group builds identity. If the group is elite, it is even better. Identity is most often created by osmosis. The more other people see you or treat you in a certain way, the more you believe that about yourself. Also you take on the identity of those who you spend time with. Receiving good coaching increases identity, and so does reviewing your successes and results.

CHAPTER 12

CREATING AND USING THE ELEMENTS AS A SYSTEM

You have now finished learning the basics of the individual elements, and you have hopefully used some of the wisdom from this Unprecedented Elemental Reality System to help in your immediate life. Good job! But we are not done yet. We still have the spiritual domain to explore, which is the most fun, inspiring, and empowering part of this training program. Before we relish the beauty and bliss of the spiritual, we have one more vital chapter in your training of my Unprecedented Elemental Reality System. To get the most from and fully understand this chapter refer to the Elementals Spectrum image in you bonus section, *eternaldharmabook.com/bonus*

All Elements Work Together in Harmony

To know each of the elements, as you do, is helpful, but the most power is accessed when you can use all the elements together, at once, in a perfect, harmonious "power blast."

The elements don't exist alone; they are always together in different proportions. You have all of the eight elements in your body, and even other things that are predominated by a particular element, such as rocks or water, also have all the other elements present within them. Therefore the first course of action to strive for in effective living is to always have all the elements fully present and in proper balance. Too much or too little of an element in any object or situation is out of alignment with dharma and therefore will be ineffective and cause suffering. Therefore if you are managing a business, make sure all the elements are present and in balance. The same goes for your relationships, health plan, football strategy, and anything else you are managing or want to enhance.

Dharma and the Elements

Everything in existence is a combination of the elements. What differentiates one object from another are the amount of each element present within it and how the elements are composed together. Therefore the key in effective action is to have the elements, in whatever you are working with, be balanced in correct proportion. When the composition and proportion of the elements are correct then dharma is present. There is no one size fits all, and that's why it is fundamentally crucial to know the dharma of whatever you are working with. If you are building a fire, too much water is harmful, but at the same time some water must be there to contain the fire or it will burn everything down. If you are building a snowman, some fire/heat is necessary, but too much will spoil the project. Everything in effective living is about finding and aligning with dharma. Therefore, if you always strive to align everything with dharma you will be the happiest and most effective person around.

The Subtle Creates the Physical

I have previously stated that the subtle creates the physical, but have not gone into much depth about it yet. It is extremely important to know how the subtle creates the physical if you are going to be powerful and effective, so we will explore it deeply in this chapter.

Anything that exists first started in the subtle domain and then condensed into the physical. Diseases start in the subtle body, then move to the energetic body, and then to the physical body. Buildings start as an inspiration, then move to plans, and then to brick and mortar. Fights start with anger or envy, and then move to the physical. There is no exception to this principle; it is just the way that reality works. Things are first subtle, then they become physical. The physical is simply a reflection, expression, and condensation of the subtle.

The exciting thing is that creation happens step-by-step through the elemental spectrum, and you already know the elements. When things are being created there may be an imbalance or "malfunction" on a particular stage of the creation process. With your knowledge of the elements you will be able to tweak the problematic element and correct any issue. You can then powerfully create anything or, even better, serve and assist the Divine in creating beautiful things.

Contemplation: Think of something that you have made. It could be an art project, a good meal, relationship, or a business. Think of how it started and observe how it was initially subtle before it became physical. Was it an inspiration, a motivation, or a fear that got you started? Or was it just some actions you took as a natural expression of who you were (identity)?

Quick Tip: If you want to understand someone's subtle reality (meaning their desires, identity, intelligence, emotions), look at their physical reality. A scattered desk means a scattered consciousness. A relaxed body means a tranquil mind. A successful entrepreneur means a focused and driven identity. Someone who likes yoga will wear yoga pants.

There are some popular ideas out there, such as the law of attraction and the Secret. They're cool, but what you are about to learn is not any of those philosophies. I find that these popular ideas often showcase some aspects of how all of reality works, and therefore can be very helpful, but they often lack sophistication and a deep understanding and grounding in the complete nature of reality, and therefore are limited in effectiveness.

The 9 Stages of Manifestation

Stage 1: Desire

My dear friend, we have not spoken in depth about desire, though it is more subtle and powerful than all the elements. Desire is not an element; it is you. The soul is made of desire and is above all the elements. It is due to your desires that you are covered with the eight elements in the form of your subtle and physical bodies.

Desire is always the first stage in any type of creation. It is the only true and real originating factor of anything.

God is also made of desire and therefore fits into this category. In the next chapter we start the third and most important part of this book: the Dharma of the Divine. In this section we will explore the nature of the soul and the divine. But for now know that the first impulse of energy that causes anything to start to manifest is desire. Here are several examples of what happens in the process of creation in each stage.

EXAMPLE 1: MOVING YOUR ARM TO SCRATCH YOUR HEAD

You have an itch on your head. More specifically, you physical body has an itch on its head and because you identify with it you feel that it's your head. You desire for the itch to be gone, so the initial energetic impulse is sent from your soul through the elemental spectrum.

EXAMPLE 2: CREATING A BUSINESS

You want the freedom from a job or to fulfil a mission, and/or money.

Quick Tip: Don't do or try to create something unless you really want to. If your desire is not strong enough there will not be enough "energetic fuel" to support creation through each of the elements. Desire is superior to the elements and therefore can control and increase them. The elements lose shape and disintegrate into chaos when they are not guided and supported by desire. This notion is known as "entropy."

Note: We as living entities do on a small scale what God does on a large scale. In the Bhagavad-Gita it states that the Divine is like a thread and everything in existence are like pearls. Just as a thread holds a necklace together, the beautiful and sweet Divine, though unseen, sustains everything in existence. It is the supreme desire of the Divine that permeates all things and thus keeps order in the Universe.

Stage 2: False Ego/Identity

The energetic impulse of desire gets filtered into the ego/identity. If the identity permits, the action continues. If it does not, it stops there.

An example of the impulse of desire being stopped at identity is if a poor man has the desire to eat at a five-star restaurant. His ego/identity may say that he is too poor to eat there, and the intelligence, which is the next stage in creation, will never be engaged in figuring out what day to make a reservation, what clothes to wear, and how much to pay the valet. He has already written of the possibility, because the desire does not match the identity, so the intelligence is never activated. Another man of the same meager financial situation may also have the desire to eat at the fancy hotel but not be prevented by the lack of sufficient identity and will use his intelligence to figure out a way.

EXAMPLE 1: MOVING YOUR ARM TO SCRATCH YOUR HEAD

Identity says, I have an arm, I have a head, and, yes, I am capable of scratching it (i.e., I am not paralyzed, in handcuffs etc.).

Example 2 (continued): Creating a Business

Identity says, "I can do this." "I am capable of building a business." I am competent.

> Quick Tip: Expand your vision. The more you believe in yourself, the more you can create. If you think you can only do something small, you will. If you think you can do something great, you will. What you need to do to create great thing is have a larger-than-life identity; you will need this reserves of energy when things get tough.

Stage 3: Intelligence/Information

On this stage of creation, information becomes apparent or actual thinking is done.

Example 1: Moving Your Arm to Scratch Your Head

The intelligence calculates the distance from your hand to your head, and figures out what angle to move in to reach the itch.

Example 2: Creating a Business

You think of business ideas, or strategy, or you learn more the about the business. You then decide which business is the best option and create a plan.

> Quick Tip: This is the second-most subtle element. Don't skimp on it. Use as much intelligence as possible in whatever you are creating. The more you think things through the better you will be able to accomplish them.

Stage 4: Mind/Emotions

The emotions must permit an action. If the emotions don't, the action cannot take place. The best creation happens when the emotions don't only allow the creation but also get obsessed with it.

EXAMPLE 1: MOVING YOUR ARM TO SCRATCH YOUR HEAD

This is a simple action. But if your emotions don't permit it, you will not do it. Have you ever been in a social situation where it would be embarrassing to pick your nose or scratch your head, even though the desire and urge is there and you know you can get away with it? You don't do it because the mind's fear of embarrassment stops you.

EXAMPLE 2: CREATING A BUSINESS

Your mind begins to echo different ideas and possibilities for the business. You get excited for success, and you may also feel that creating such a business is a daunting process.

> Quick Tip: Put passion into it. People often speak of the need to put passion into your actions and they are right. A healthy passion and upbeat motivation to create is a supportive mind element. Actions that are infused with inspired emotions are more effective.

Stage 5: Ether/Sound/Space

Sound/ether/space comes as communication, the actual physical space, and the initial vibrational mantra that moves air, as I described in Chapter 8.

EXAMPLE 1: MOVING YOUR ARM TO SCRATCH YOUR HEAD

The sound-like vibration begins to vibrate to direct the air/prana/chi to flow.

EXAMPLE 2: CREATING A BUSINESS

You begin to talk to investors, mentors, partners, and potential customers.

> Quick Tip: For power in project-creating, communicate, communicate, communicate. The more ether, sound, and communication, the more power. Space and sound expressed as proximity and communication are what connect individuals, and a project is all about connecting people together for a fruitful result.

Stage 6: Air/Chi/Prana/Energy

Raw power is allocated and accumulated for the upcoming action, and/or air energy begins to move.

EXAMPLE 1: MOVING YOUR ARM TO SCRATCH YOUR HEAD

The energy in your arm begins to flow in the direction of your head. For movement to happen, air has to move first. When it moves, other physical things follow. In practical life this all happens instantaneously as if it is one action.

EXAMPLE 2: CREATING A BUSINESS

You get the funds, tools, and other raw materials (such as lemons for you lemonade stand) to start the business. You get this from the people who you were communicating with in the ether stage.

Stage 7: Fire

Fire is seen as the burning of energy that moves physical objects and therefore is action. It is not just cars that burn energy to move. Fire can also take the form of electrical currents in the nerves that send the message to move.

Example 1: Moving Your Arm to Scratch Your Head

Due to the movement of chi/prana/air, the nerves start to send electrical currents and messages ordering the arm to move.

Calories are burnt to release the energy needed to move the arm.

Example 2. Creating a Business

You start to set up and run the business. You begin burning investment funds and other energy previously acquired to compile and operate the business. You squeeze your lemons for your lemonade.

> Quick Tip: Fire is action. You must act to create. (You'd be surprised how many people don't get that.)

Stage 8: Water

Adaptation and innovation are needed to create the final result. Water nourishes earth, so in this stage nourishment is given.

Example 1: Moving Your Arm to Scratch Your Head

The blood and other juices (water) of the body begin to move. They supply the muscles and tissues with nourishment and lubrication to move.

Example 2. Creating a Business

You adapt your strategy according to the market, the demand, and your competition. The world is always changing, and you never have it 100-percent right the first time, so you must adapt and adjust to reach the final results.

You nourish and care for your assets such as funds, prospects, tools, and networks.

> Quick Tip: I heard a great business teacher once say that plans always change but planning is indispensable. Always be ready to adapt you final plan, because the world is always changing. At the same time try you best to make a plan that is so complete that it needs no adaptation.

Stage 9: Earth

Earth appears as systems, structures, habits, and final established results.

EXAMPLE 1: MOVING YOUR ARM TO SCRATCH YOUR HEAD

Your physical arm moves from the force of the other elements and you scratch your head.

Your tangible result has been achieved.

EXAMPLE 2: CREATING A BUSINESS

You put systems in place to keep it running consistently. Profits roll in. You now have an established business.

> Quick Tip 1: To maintain tangible results, systems, which are earthlike, are key. Build strong and powerful systems. Earth is simple so you want your systems to be simple, overly complicated systems tend to crumble faster.
>
> Quick Tip 2: Use the qualities of water to deal with many of the day-to-day trials that show up in your project. You can't be effective if you are too preemptive in your systematizing. You need to flow (water) with everything before you can systematize it (earth). If you are ready to dance and flow, you can lead everything to a solid conclusion and then lock it away in a safe, steady system.

Your Job as Creator and Manager

As a manager of the elements and a steward of creation, it is your job to find where there is a blockage in the creation process, which means to find in which element there is a lack or an excess. You need to make sure that there is an appropriate balance of the element in accordance to the dharma of what you are working with. This means that each element exists in the correct proportions. I know this can be tough, but you'll get good at this; you know a lot now. You can get hyper analytical and technical with this, or you can be laid back and just notice when the energy of an element is missing as you flow through life and give it some attention to put things back on track.

3 Ways to "Manipulate" the Elements

1. The Element Itself

You can increase or decrease or manipulate any element by working directly with it. This is done by consciously imbibing the attributes of the element or negating it. As you will learn in the next chapter, desire is part of the soul and therefore more powerful than the elements. Simply by being aware of something and focusing on it you can start to affect it. For example, if you want more of the steadiness of earth, create systems.

2. The Element Before It on the Element Spectrum

Go to the subtle element before it in the spectrum to increase the element. Increase air to increase fire, for example. Here's a practical example: If you want more steadiness of earth, adapt like water to find the right systems that work. For even better results, enhance all the elements on the spectrum that come before it. For example, you need more of the raw power of air, so you increase ether, mind, intelligence ego/identity, and desire.

The Element After It on the Element Spectrum

Go to the more physical element that comes next on the spectrum to decrease the more subtle element before it. In other words, increase fire to decrease air. Here a practical example: You have too much passion, drive, and vision of fire such that it is devouring you. Increase the tenderness and going-with-the-flow-ness of water. The more physical elements on the spectrum, generally decrease the more subtle ones before it, because the physical is a condensation of the subtle—yet still the physical supports and affects the subtle: Earth provides the structure and support for water to flow, and air provides support for the vocal chords used for making sound in ether. You can use all the more physical elements that come later on the spectrum to support a particular element. Use all the other elements to cement a new identity.

Sequence in Creating

Because creation happens from subtle to physical, you want to start with the subtle elements when you are creating. First ascertain your dharma, then explore and clarify your desires (soul), then create identity, then think of possibilities and strategies and create a plan (intelligence), then invest feelings into it and absorb your mind and consciousness, then communicate the inspiration (desire), plan (intelligence), and feelings (mind) to your supporters, then gather the ingredients needed (air), then start using them and physically creating with enthusiasm, passion, and drive (fire), then adapt to the natural flux of the Universe, dance and increase flow (water). Once you have found a formula that works and is tested, repeat that steadily (earth). There you have it—that's how to create powerfully.

A Natural Yearning to Connect

I am about to share with you something that I find quite beautiful. I used to speak about this when teaching in the remote villages of Bengal, which, according to the *Guinness Book of World Records*, was "the most likely place in the world to be eaten by a tiger." When I was in my early 20s, my Guru sent me into small Bengali villages to teach. My team and I lived in mud huts and traveled, often by foot, from village to village. In my mind's eye I can still feel the warm, affectionate glances of the elderly village folk as they huddled around me to hear the class. These classes were often lighted by kerosene lamps or candles because villagers had no running water or electricity. In this sweet setting I would often explain the following concept.

Each element is always yearning and naturally strives to connect with its source. If you drop earth, gravity pulls it to its origin, the greater mass of earth. If you observe water you can see that it is always looking to find the shortest path to the ocean. Fire flares up to connect with the sun, and when air is submerged it bubbles up to connect with the totality of air. In the same way, the soul is always striving to connect with conscious love. That's why humans are social animals and always seeking to connect with other living beings. But we will only be fully content when connected with the source of all love and consciousness: the Divine.

Relax and Flow

From this notion we find that the elements also have a way of naturally acting without our force or influence. Our job, then, becomes much easier: All we need to do is know how the elements are naturally flowing and flow with them. But what does this mean? It could sound like I am giving conflicting information. On one hand, I am saying to dominate and control the elements: That's what you need to do to take charge, create, and make things happen. But on the other hand it may seem like I am saying to be passive: Don't act because the elements are flowing and "doing their thing" without you. I have also previously stated that God makes all things happen; He/She is actually doing everything, and most of what we think we are doing or can do is an illusion. So how do we live and interact with the world if we are going to be effective and evolve spiritually on our path to Passionate Enlightenment?

2 Paths to Power and Inner Inspiration

Some time ago I was swimming in the ocean and was contemplating one section of the Bhagavad-Gita (one of the most important Vedic texts) that says that there are two types of people. It says some people are Godly while others are demoniac.

I never liked or understood this. To me it sounded like the black-and-white, binary way of thinking that many religious extremists use to justify mistreating other human beings while sitting on a high horse with an egoic sense of superiority. Philosophically I don't believe in an objective good and bad. I believe that what is right for one person may be wrong for another. If a civilian kills someone it is wrong and society has repercussions for such wrongdoing, whereas if a military man kills many people he may be promoted, rewarded, and respected. This principle is everywhere in life, and in the Vedic approach, one man's poison is another man's medicine. One of the great things about the concept of dharma is that it teaches that we all have unique, personal individual purpose and duty. I would even controversially say that we also have an individual measure of morality. Yet the scripture that is so dear to my heart and has brought me peace, love, light, and clarity in my darkest times, seemed to be propounding this black-and-white objective, binary, absolutist psychology.

As I was contemplating all of this, I felt a spiritual blessing from my beloved Lord, and I felt that inner knowledge known as Veda sprout within me, and it all made sense. Everything became clear and my heart was profoundly touched.

Such internal blessings and inspirations are available to everyone. Such inner love and guidance are not only reserved for prophets and messiahs but are the birthright of all living beings. I am writing this book with the sole purpose to help you passionately connect with the Divine and teach you to tune into His/Her constant support and guidance.

Choose Your Path

It is not that there are two types of people but that there are two basic ways in which we can approach life and relate to it. On one path you think that you are the owner and controller of all things; you see that the world is your oyster and that you need to manipulate the energy of this world and take what you want. The other path says there is a divine power superior to you; your primary focus is in creating a loving relationship with that power. On this path you also "manipulate" the elements and act with vigor, passion, and purpose, but the action is selfless and done out of love. The happiness, joy, and contentment that you experience from acting in loving service to the divine are greater than any happiness that you could experience from enjoying the fruits of your labor. Another way of saying this is that there is more joy in creating and managing anything, such as a home, company, or kingdom under the direction of the Divine, than there is in doing the exact same things to enjoy it all for yourself.

Both paths work. With either path you can create empires, become rich, and be effective in what you do, yet there is a clear and distinct energy, motivation, experience, and final result for each path. The easiest way to describe this would be to say that one is light while the other is dark.

The Dark Path to Power

This path is dominated by selfishness and the desire to enjoy. One who travels this path tries to own and control everything. The focus on this path is inward, and when walking this path you could care less about other people; you simply want to gratify your own urges. This selfishness closes and hardens your heart. On the dark path you have no space for other people in your heart because your ever-increasing desires are unmet, so you feel that you first should satisfy yourself before you can think of others. This is impossible, because your desires are always growing and the soul can't be satisfied by the elements of this world anyway. As you progress down this path, you regard others less and less, to the point where you can kill and rape for your own ends. History is littered with stories of war and abuse by those who choose this path.

In the next chapter you will learn more about the soul. But for now know that as a spirit soul we have a certain degree of power that enables us to control nature and the elements. Therefore with enough strong focus, identity, and desire we can effectively amass a great amount of wealth and power, even when walking the dark path to power.

The Shining Path to Power

In contrast, when you walk the shining path to power, your attention is focused outward. You are not thinking about your needs and wants; you are thinking about others' needs and applying your energy there. By caring for and helping others, they are in turn inspired to care for and help you and thus your needs are also met.

This "giving first" model is the new marketing trend; it just works better.

Love is inherently satisfying. The soul strives for it. Love is selfless by nature, and that's why if you do "an act of love" to manipulate and secretly want something in return, people can feel it and the sweetness is lost. There is no love in such action. When you choose the shining path to power, you don't want anything in return and people feel it. Their heart melts and they strive to give back and love you in return. Your life then becomes a constant giving and receiving of love, which leads to even more happiness, power, and joy.

One who truly walks the Shining Path to Power is always seeking to serve selflessly, and therefore their intelligence is not deluded by lust, anger, or greed. They are thus able to make better clear-headed decisions. These clear-headed decisions and the genuine support from others enable them to progress much further than those on the dark path, and this is not taking God's support into account nor the eternal principle of karma.

God's Support

God is not just some elusive machine that lives in the sky. He/She is also a person with feelings and also has a need for love. When you love Him/Her, His heart also melts and He supports you in everything you do. God is all-powerful by definition, so it can be a plus to have Him/Her on your side.

We will explore the dharma and nature of you, the soul, in the next chapter and the dharma of the Divine in the chapter after that, but for now suffice it to say that the Eternal Dharma of the soul is to be selflessly serving in a constant love-play with the Divine. When playing this love-play you are always looking for ways to serve and please the Divine.

God is present everywhere, and so is His guidance and His will. Therefore when walking the shining path to power you are constantly tuning in to the all-pervading and constant pulsating desire of the Supreme that vibrates through all elements. When the Divine guides you, you are never lost. You always know what to do, because you have access to all the knowledge of the Universe, and thus you act in the most effective and love imbued way possible.

Karma

The eternal principle of karma is simple: It simply means that every action has a reaction. Karma says that if you do good stuff, good stuff will happen to you; and if you do bad stuff to others, bad stuff will happen to you. By nature, the dark path to power leads you to harming others and the shining path to power leads you to helping others. So when following the shining path to power, you start getting lots of good luck and support from others, and many good things start happening to you.

We All Walk Both Paths

The fact that we are bound by and identify with our two bodies indicates that we walk both paths, and we generally oscillate between them. If we only walked the shining path we would be fully enlightened and transcend beyond this limiting world of the elements. If we walked only the dark path, we would have such bad karma and such a dark energy to us that after briefly enjoying whatever we create, we would probably die, or worse. The fact that you are reading this book is a clear indication that you walk the shining path more than most.

Suffering With God Syndrome?

The fact that we are not fully enlightened shows that we have some degree of God Syndrome. Therefore, even though we want only to walk the shining path, our past habits and our unenlightened-ness will have us sometimes act by the principles of the dark path. Some spiritual teachings like to propagate the feeling of guilt to deal with this. I disagree with this. I say it's best just to understand and accept it for what it is; still love yourself, God, and all beings; and continue forward to the best of your ability. By walking the shining path as much as you can, you will get better at it, so shine on, my friend!

How to Walk the Shining Path

1. Choose to walk it, for everything is born of choice.
2. Always look for what others need and how you can serve, support, and help. Remember to act on what you find.
3. Whenever dealing with an element and the things of this world, still your mind, and gently tune in and listen. The pulsating desire of the Divine exists everywhere, and if you tune in you can hear it. Once you hear it, follow that Divine guidance with all your heart. The Vedic culture repeatedly stresses the importance of having a guru. The reason for this is because the guru can tune in and hear the will of the Divine better than someone who is less practiced and advanced. Therefore it is vital for any serious spiritual practitioner to take the shelter of a guru and receive their guidance. Sadly it is hard to find a truly selfless and enlightened guru; most gurus have some type of selfish interest, but don't let

this deter you. If you are sincere, the Divine will arrange the right guide for you in your spiritual evolution.

4. Do the Mantra Meditation and other spiritual practices outlined in this book. They are all designed to help you tune in to the will of the supreme and walk this shining path.

PART 3

THE DHARMA
OF THE DIVINE

CHAPTER 13

The Constitutional Nature of the Soul: Dharma of the Soul

We are now starting the final and most important section of the book. In Part 1 you learned several Vedic foundational principles such as dharma. In Part 2 you learned the Unprecedented Elemental Reality System that if used will empower you in any field of life, be it personal growth, Effective Action, or even love, business, and war. Now in Part 3 we explore the juiciest wisdom of them all: We learn the dharma of the Spiritual Domain.

The Spiritual Domain = Most Subtle

The spiritual domain consists of you, the soul, and the divine. It is far more subtle than any of the elements and therefore it is more important and powerful. At the same time, due to its subtle nature, it is significantly harder to perceive. Just as through practice you can perceive and interact with the more subtle elements of nature, you can also perceive and interact with the spiritual domain with the right amount of practice; and by doing so you not only have a happier, more joyous experience while you live and act in your day-to-day life, you also can be more powerful because your actions become imbued with poise, love, tranquility, and passion.

Some people may say that because they can't see the spiritual domain it does not exist. To those who have experienced it or who regularly operate in that domain, it sounds naïve. It sounds like someone is saying that just because they don't see radio waves, nuclear energy, or wi-fi that it does not exist.

The Story of the Frog in the Well

Once upon a time there were two frogs in a well. One frog had never left the well. To him the well was all in all, and there was nothing more to know. The other frog had explored significantly beyond the well and had even witnessed the vast ocean. The traveler frog was trying to tell the stationary frog of the vast reality beyond the well and the stationary frog was not having it. The traveler frog said that there was a body of water called the ocean that was millions of times bigger than the puddle in their old well. The stationary frog claimed that this was impossible; how could there be anything greater than the mighty puddle in his well? He had not seen anything beyond it and therefore concluded that there was nothing beyond it.

Human beings often have the same psychology as the frog in the well. Due to God Syndrome they feel that their limited experience is all in all. Therefore they doubt any notion that is outside of their realm of experience, such as the subtle elements or the spiritual domain.

It can be scary to acknowledge that our notion of reality is incomplete, and therefore ignorance provides us a kind of bliss. By not acknowledging the unknown we limit our perspective on what is and is not true, and thus we limit our effectiveness. I sometimes catch myself thinking with the same psychology as the frog in the well, and I intentionally remove that limiting thought process from my mind.

Contemplation Exercise

Think of at least three times when your thinking was small—when your ego felt that you understood everything when in fact you did not. When have you disregarded information based on your subjective and limited experience? In truth we are very small; we have limited understanding of all the millions upon millions of galaxies and planets in the Universe. I know it does not feel good to contemplate your minuteness and limited knowledge, but it is important to sometimes do this so you can see things as they actually are so that you can grow and learn.

The Big Question

The great philosophers, intellectuals, and spiritual legends of history have all asked the question: Who am I? There are many right answers to this question, and we all have some notion of self-identity. I find that the 5,000-year-old Vedic wisdom provides such a detailed level of wisdom on this subject that is so sweet, inspiring, and empowering that I have to share it with you. This knowledge of the Spiritual Domain, and the soul, is an intertwined and an integral part of the Unprecedented Elemental Reality System.

The answer to the big question of "Who am I?" and explanations of the spiritual domain are subjects that are also spoken about in some religions, and, though I am often considered a Hindu, my approach is not religious, it is spiritual. In more than a decade of teaching in 20 countries around the world I have not found this wisdom to clash with anyone's religious beliefs. Regardless of which religion or faith anyone subscribes to—even if it is none at all—I have always found this wisdom to work. (In the next chapter we go deeper into reconciling religion with spirituality and all this wisdom.)

You the Soul

In essence the ancient wisdom of the East says that we are a spirit soul. The soul, which is the true you, is a spark of pure consciousness that is of a superior and different nature to any of the elements. Though it is covered by the elements and identifies with them, the soul is distinct from and transcendental to them. In simple terms this means that you are not your body, nor your mind, nor your thoughts or beliefs; you are something else.

According to ancient spiritual wisdom, there are two qualities that make the soul unique and differentiate it from inert matter (the eight elements). These qualities are inherently part of us and define our very being and thus they are inseparable from the soul: independence and free will.

Independence

As living, conscious beings we have certain power. We have the ability to move, control, and manipulate the elements. Our power to do this is limited, yet we still have it. How much rein we have over the elements depends on how we focus our energy; this book is intended to help you do that better.

Even the most powerless among us, such as those who are paralyzed, still have the quality of independence and therefore have some control over the elements. For example, they may be able to blink or have some control of their identity, intelligence, and mind.

When we are fully enlightened and passionately imbued with the highest type of spiritual love, we no longer care to control the elements of this world and our quality of independence is expressed in the multitude of ways we choose to love, serve, and connect with the divine.

> **Contemplation:** Lift up your hand. Now put it down. Notice how you are not your hand: It is made of the eight elements, yet you have control over it.

Note on Responsibility: When people start the spiritual journey they learn that their power is small and that it is ego that often makes us think that we are greater than we are. They also learn that Spiritual Surrender and detachment are key parts of the spiritual journey and that everything in the Universe runs on the will of the Divine. Oftentimes people misunderstand the application of these concepts and think that to grow spiritually they must abstain from action, and that they are not responsible for their life, their actions, or their results. Many spiritual seekers become lazy and powerless because of these misconceptions, and many lazy people take to spirituality because its theory seems to support their apathy. Needless to say, it is important for us to take 100-percent responsibility for our life, choices, and actions, for the quality of independence is part of our core being. It is in our soul and therefore responsibility, power, and action are part of our Eternal Dharma. We exist to act and serve. Therefore any inaction is going directly against the core nature of our soul: It is adharmic (not dharmic).

Free Will

Just as the quality of independence is an inseparable part of the soul, so is the quality of free will. What we want is what makes us, us. Desires cannot come from an external source or be forced upon or implanted in us. People often ask me to make them want to progress spiritually, and it is something I can't do. Not even God can force someone to want anything.

Our choices can solely come from us because that power to want and choose is what defines our being; they are what differentiate us from inert matter.

Two Avenues for Free Will

We know advertising, propaganda, and social engineering are designed to make us want certain things. If this can be done then the question arises: Where is free will? The Vedas teach that our free will can be boiled down to two rudimentary desires. We can choose to be selfless and love, or we can choose to be selfish and try to enjoy separately from the divine. Another way to say this is: We can choose to look toward or away from the divine.

When we choose selfless love, we grow spiritually, and as we grow we come closer and closer to the Divine, until we are fully Passionately Enlightened. When we choose to look away and try to enjoy selfishly, we are influenced by the eight elements that cover us. The elements that cover us have a pulling of their own and therefore will influence the way in which our desire to enjoy selfishly is expressed. For example, the gender

and DNA of our physical body, combined with our age, previous experiences, social conditioning, and psychological condition, will determine
our sexual desires, such as who we are attracted to. The core desire that
originated from the soul was to enjoy separately from the Divine and,
because we identify with the eight elements, they shaped the expression of
that core desire. Advertising works on the subtle body (mind, intelligence,
ego) and attempts to shape and influence. Therefore it affects us.

Desire

In the Elemental Reality System I simply call both qualities—independence
and free will—desire. Desire is a simple yet accurate way to understand
who we are or what the soul is.

Desire is more subtle to the elements and therefore is the most powerful force: All the Elements are useless and functionless when they are not
guided by desire. So choose well, my friend; you are powerful.

Two Qualities and Love

Desire is what makes love, love. Without desire it is slavery. The whole
beauty of love lies in free will and selfless giving. We suffer in this world
because we are not connected in love. It is our Eternal Dharma to be in
a constant, loving union with the divine, but, even though it's our birthright, our constitutional position, and our dharma to live in the rapture of
eternal love, we are still able to suffer in this world because love is a choice
and we can choose not to give it.

The subject of suffering in this world is a large and often deeply emotional one. Know that we can choose eternal happiness through selfless
love to the Divine, or we can choose to try to separately enjoy in this
world. This generally ends in suffering because such worldly endeavors
are not our dharma.

The sweet thing about selfless, pure, passionate spiritual love is that
the Divine becomes bound by it and, even though the Divine is the origin
of all of existence and the master of all creation, the love that is part of our
soul dominates Him/Her. The Divine is thirsty and eager for the sweetness of the love that rests in our hearts.

The Divine and the Soul Are Made of the Same Things

The soul and the Divine are actually the same in quality: They both have independence and free will. But the quantity is different. Just as a drop of ocean water has the same qualities as the vast ocean, yet there is a world of difference between the two, in the same way the soul has the same qualities as God, yet there is still a world of difference. You have a minute amount of the independence and free will, whereas God or the Divine has an infinite amount. For example, the quality of independence enables us to control our bodies to do our jobs, create businesses, and function with our friends and families. The quality of independence in the divine enables Him or Her to create all the Universes, galaxies, atoms, and all other things in existence.

> **Contemplation:** Think of at least three times when you wanted something that you were not supposed to, but you still wanted it anyway. This is your free will.

What Is the Soul Made Of?

There is more to the soul than just the two qualities of independence and free will. According to the 5,000-year-old spiritual wisdom and the experience of countless spiritual practitioners, just as the material world is made of eight elements, the spiritual domain, which includes you the soul, is made of three "elements" or energies. These energies are known as Sat, Chit, and Ananda in Sanskrit, which I like to translate as being, knowing, and loving. Just as learning the elements empowers us to better use them to be more effective and to attain Passionate Enlightenment, learning what the soul is made of also empowers us.

Being = Eternal Existence

This first potency that is inherently part of the spiritual domain, and therefore you, is the existence potency. Existence is the energy that is life; it is the energy that causes you to be. It is the very notion and fact of being or existing. Basically this energy is what allows you to exist. Without it there would be no you.

A key factor of the existence potency is eternality. True existence is eternal, and it is never destroyed. Our bodies will one day be destroyed, yet we never want to die. Death is unnatural and adharmic (not dharmic) for the soul, and we only experience it because we falsely identify with this temporary body. When we are fully enlightened and exist in our fullest spiritual potential, we live forever in our spiritual form and will not suffer the pain of death ever again.

The Most Amazing Fact

Once upon a time the legendary King Yudhistira of India was roaming the forest in search of water. He came across a lake, where he found his four brothers all appearing to be dead. The mystical creature in charge of the lake appeared and demanded he correctly answer several questions in order to bring his brothers back to life.

Of the many questions asked by the creature, one prominent question was "What is the most amazing fact?" Yudhistira replied, "The most amazing fact is that though everyone must die and we see death around us at all times, we all think that we will not die."

The creature thus satisfied by King Yudhistira's answers brought the brothers back to life and let them drink from his lake.

Contemplation: Think of at least three movies, stories, or personal experiences that reflect the innate desire to live. I always find it interesting to see how movies show people striving to live against all odds. I believe this desire to live eternally originates from the existence, or being, potency of the soul. We all want to live forever.

Knowing

Knowing—a consciousness, an awareness, and a cognitive intelligence—is one of the potencies of the soul. As the famous Latin philosopher Rene Descartes said, "I think, therefore I am."

This potency can be seen as a higher knowing that exists within us. The fun of this is that when you connect with your inner self you can find all the knowledge and wisdom you would ever need. In Chapter 1 I explained this when teaching the concept of Veda. This knowing potency of the soul is pretty much the same energy as Veda. We could get more philosophical about it, but simply knowing that there is a higher knowledge eternally present in the soul is enough for now.

When we are conditioned in this world by identifying with our bodies, this knowing potency is expressed as knowledge of the things of this world. When we are Passionately Enlightened this knowledge potency is expressed as direct knowledge of our relationship with the divine, and it is beautiful, my friend.

It is important to note that this innate spiritual knowledge of the soul is composed of a completely different substance to the information of the intelligence element or the feelings of the mind. These types of knowledge cannot be compared to each other: One is hard data and the other is a spiritual experience of our highest self, known as our soul.

Contemplation: Think of at least three times when you have felt an inner truth. Notice how you knew something that you should not have known. This intuition or inner knowledge was likely an expression of the knowledge potency of the soul. Yes, it could have just been your mind reflecting information and feelings back, or it could have been calculations of your intelligence, but I bet there is at least one time in which you felt such strong inner truth or gut feeling that was clearly not your mind or intelligence. It was something else.

Doing the spiritual meditations and practices in this book help you with defining and refining this inner knowing. I trust that with sincere practice you will get good at this.

Loving/Bliss/Joy

My favorite of the potencies of the Divine is this one: the potency of Loving or, as I like to see it, flavor. This energy is often called bliss because it's the fun one; literally, it is this energy that causes fun, happiness, joy, and pleasure to be. Without it there would be no fun. According to the wisdom of the ancients, joy is part of the soul. We exist as joyful beings. We strive for joy; joy is our dharma, our constitutional nature, and our duty.

This innate bliss-joy-love is within us at all times, and by doing meditation and basically calming the subtle body, which means stopping the mind and intelligence and ego from distracting us, we can feel this joy that requires no external stimulus. You can sometimes feel it when you are alone and at peace.

Many spiritual practices are meant to lead us to this place of inner peace and inner contentment. But, such inner peace is just the beginning. The highest type of joy does not happen when you are alone: It exists in a spiritual love exchange with the Divine. Let me explain.

The Seed Must Sprout

When you identify with your two bodies (physical and subtle), these three potencies of the soul—being, knowing, and loving—exist like a seed waiting to sprout. When you are fully Passionately Enlightened, these three potencies are like a fully grown tree that is blooming with fragrant fruits and flowers.

Many spiritual processes strive to stop the seed from being influenced by the covering of the two bodies, and allow the seed to exist in its pure, unhampered glory. These spiritual processes clean the seed from the influence of this world and thus you find peace and bliss, but they don't plant it to grow to its fullest potential. Such a "clean seed" state of being is a type of enlightenment, and is very hard and rare to achieve. This type of enlightenment is good, and will destroy stuffing and grant you inner pleasure and peace. Passionate Enlightenment, on the other hand, is even more rare, and it is not simply about destroying suffering and being at peace; it is about planting and growing the seed to connect in love with the divine and eternally dance in cosmic love-play. Passionate Enlightenment is the fully blossomed tree.

Just as a seed takes time to sprout, take root, grow, and blossom, so it takes time, practice, and continual nourishment to grow into a state of pure passionate spiritual love with the Divine. The beginning of the spiritual process is often the hardest, God Syndrome holds us tight, and selfishness keeps us bound, but as we do our Mantra Meditation, follow our dharmas, and continually learn, Enlightened Action becomes easier and easier and sweeter and sweeter—to the point of a spiritual addiction to the divine and our seed-like potential of love blossoms into a sturdy and beautiful tree.

> **Contemplation:** Think of three things that you have done in the last 24 hours in order to get love and/or feel a type of joy. Then contemplate about how much your entire life has been about finding happiness, joy, love, and beauty. This is all the Loving potency of the soul.

Our Eternal Dharma

Now you know what the soul is made of, but what does it do? What is its purpose—its dharma?

Just as different kinds of seeds grow to into different types of trees, enlightenment is not "one size fits all." Each soul has a different Eternal Dharma, which means that we all have a unique and special relationship with the Divine. Each of us has a different eternal form (being), a different relationship with the Divine to know about (knowing), and a different bliss to feel in that relationship (loving). This means that our love and value cannot be duplicated, and therefore we each have a unique special individual place in the Universe that no one else can fill. The Divine needs us just as we need Him/Her.

Though each of our dharmas is unique, there are a few common traits that all of us share.

Service

The first quality of everyone's Eternal Dharma is service. I know this does not sound fun; our God Syndrome freaks out when we here this. But in actuality there is far more pleasure in service, when done properly, than there is in any other action.

Service means that we are active participants in a love exchange. We don't just simply sit passively in enlightenment; we act, we do, and we flow. In such action the third potency of the soul, bliss/joy/love is activated. Through this service-action love is churned, increased, and extracted, and our soul is nourished by the supremely sweet nectar. When a mother is breastfeeding her child, who is serving and who is served? And which one is getting more happiness in the interaction? Though the mother is serving and the child is being served, more often than not, it is the mother that is enjoying the interaction more. This is because in a loving interacting there is more joy serving with love than there is in being served. Therefore, our Eternal Dharma of servitude affords us access to the greatest type of joy, pleasure, and happiness.

> **Contemplation:** Service is an inseparable part of our soul; it is part of our Eternal Dharma. When we identify with our two bodies—the subtle and the physical—our dharma is not fully expressed, yet it is still there.
>
> Think of at least three examples of how everyone is always serving and cannot stop, no matter how much they may try or how much of a master they think they are. For example, a CEO serves investors and customers. A king serves his citizens and wife. A celebrity serves her dog by walking him or her. A president serves his or her children.
>
> Everyone must always serve, so I say: Why not choose to serve the Divine?

Spiritual Surrender

The next aspect of everyone's Eternal Dharma is Spiritual Surrender. I touched upon this when describing the Shining Path to Power at the end of the last chapter.

Spiritual Surrender is characterized by letting the Divine take charge. It's about following the lead of the Divine and acting according to His or Her will. Our practice and aim on the spiritual path is to always follow the guidance of the Divine, in every action we do and every thought we think. Again I know that our God Syndrome does not like to hear that, because we sometimes think that it is somehow a lower position to be of service and to follow a lead. This is so far from the truth.

Divine Salsa

In salsa dancing one partner, generally the man, leads and the other partner, generally the woman, follows. There is a loving communication between both dancers, yet still the leader chooses and decides how the dance will go. The follower yields and adapts to the direction of the lead. The follower surrenders, the lead guides, and magic is made.

The Divine pervades all things at all times. To walk the path of enlightenment. All you need to do is practice spiritually surrendering and follow the lead of the Divine. From there the rest is taken care of.

Once we have gotten good at dancing with the Divine through Spiritual Surrender, it gets more and more fun, to the point where our whole being is inundated with bliss and we eternally live an exciting ever-fresh cosmic spiritual dancing love affair with the Divine.

I know this may seem far-fetched or too theoretical and abstract to understand. It is super subtle and hard to perceive, and, as you know, that is why there is so much power in it.

Being of constant service, surrendering spiritually, and attempting to tune into the will of the divine to guide your actions are not just the keys to Passionate Enlightenment; such practices will also make you the most effective in producing tangible, measurable results.

These actions are of the soul, which is the most subtle thing that fuels power into the rest of the elements. The soul (desire) creates ego/identity, which creates intelligence, which creates the mind/emotions, all the way down to the tangible results of earth.

If you continue to practice the Mantra Meditations outlined in this book, especially the upcoming Mantra Meditation practice, plus you continue to bring awareness to this by learning more (*www.vishnu-swami. com* can help with that), I promise you that this wisdom and spiritual experience will gradually unfold in your heart and the bliss, sweetness, and serenity of the spiritual domain will be yours.

CHAPTER 14

THE 3 STAGES OF SPIRITUAL EVOLUTION

In this chapter I will facilitate you in getting full clarity on spirituality and religion and how it affects you. In the next chapter we will get full clarity on what is known as the Divine, Spirit, or God. These subjects are vital if we are to actually attain enlightenment, and therefore I must speak concretely rather than in a way that is ambiguous and politically safe, and I am aware that the subject of the Divine religion or God can be a touchy subject to some. I will keep it fun and light while at the same time speaking concretely and introducing new concepts that will bring you so much clarity and peace on your path to enlightenment.

I am not preaching any one religious doctrine, and I don't intend to disrespect anyone's faith, because I truly love and respect all spiritual paths.

Foundation for Feeling Bliss

Before we get into an in-depth analysis of the Divine, we shall shed light on how people approach understanding the Divine. I want you to assimilate this knowledge into the core of your being, so that you don't just read and talk about enlightenment but actually feel its divine rapture. I want the bliss of your soul to constantly shine and your heart to sing in joy while you eternally dance with the Divine.

For this to happen and for you to fully benefit from this book, I need you to situate yourself in the third stage of Spiritual Evolution. Chances are you are already there. But you may want to keep in mind that those in the third stage can still be partially influenced by first- and second-stage mentalities.

To advance to the third stage all you have to do is simply choose to do so. It may take a little time to get there, especially with the pressures of society and the ideas that it sometimes ingrains in us, but you will get there, my friend.

The 1st Stage of Spiritual Evolution: Dogmatic Religion

The Formation

In older times people tried to understand and connect with God or the divine through religion. They related with God in ways that were familiar to them—in ways that reflected their culture, language, dress, and way of life. Over the years prophets appeared, traditions were solidified, and firm religions were established.

Undoubtedly these religions helped their followers spiritually connect and transcend the troubles of this world. Because these religions only existed in one culture and had little to no contact with other cultures they were steeped in culture and tradition. In time these externals, such as dress, language, and rituals, became inseparable from a religion and seemingly its spiritual teachings as well.

People congregated at places of worship and faith was placed in the religion and its leaders. Political opportunists and power seekers could not deny the power that religion held, so they began to infiltrate and create alliances with these religious groups.

By the participation of the faithful and the support of government, these religions became large and powerful institutions. Yet they still remained tribal, in the sense that they existed only within one culture and were a central part of the social life of the time.

My Way Is Better Than Your Way

People are naturally narcissistic and think they are superior to others. When these civilizations came in contact with other civilizations they felt that their own culture and civilization were superior and thus also thought that their own religion and their way of approaching God were better. When others challenged the culture of their faith, either directly or by following something else, people felt that they were challenging the religion's spiritual teachings. Thus both religious leaders and followers alike embraced the mentality that taught that their spiritual path was the best or only path. In time the idea of "my way is the only way" and "my God is the only God"—which really means "I am better than you"—became indistinguishable from the sweet, beautiful spiritual wisdom that the original founding prophets intended to share.

Meaning to You

Why does this matter to us? First, by understanding and contemplating the evolution of spiritual wisdom we can see how many of these ways of thinking affect our mind now. I find that even though we may not so overtly think that we are better than others or our way is the only way, these psychologies can creep in and still affect our subtle body. When we are conscious of all of this we can then consciously choose how much of these ways of thinking we want to accept.

Exercise

Ask yourself the following questions.

1.   Do I still think that my way is the only way?
2.   How superior to others do I feel due to my religious and spiritual beliefs?
3.   How much of what I believe is culturally, traditionally, and socially imposed, and how much is actually deeply spiritual?

The 2nd Stage of Spiritual Evolution: Politically Correct Spirituality

As the world progressed, so did globalization, and people began to live cross-culturally. Cultures cross-pollinated and people were no longer isolated in one culture or ethnic group. Thus their ideas of God and spirituality began to expand beyond a "my way is the only way" mentality. Just as racism was no longer politically correct, going on a superiority trip based on religion was also not.

I believe that for the most part, this is where we are as a culture now. People have come to learn to accept people of other religions. By living in a multicultural society everyone can see that those from other cultures and religions are normal, fine, and good people. Thus the second stage of Spiritual Evolution, in which all faiths are accepted and respected, and in which everyone has a right to connect with the divine in their own way and all paths are seen as equal, is upon us.

A good example and indication of this shift in mentality is seen in this quote from His Holiness, Pope Francis. I find this especially significant because in other ages the Pope would be one of those who sanctioned wars "in the name of God." Pope Francis said in his message, released January 6, 2016, the feast of the Epiphany: "Many think differently, feel differently, seeking God or meeting God in different ways. In this crowd [there were leaders from all the major religions present], in this range of religions, there is only one certainty that we have for all: we are all children of God."

Fertile Ground for Spirituality

This openness to many religions has laid fertile ground to the growth of Spirituality. Spirituality is a way of connecting with God (the Divine) without submitting to a religious institution, or being confined to the approach of any one tradition or culture. Spirituality is ideal for many because it is very politically correct, by being "not religious, but spiritual" you don't step on anybody's toes and you get to eat from the global buffet of spiritual styles and paths.

As I mentioned previously, I believe that the majority of modern society is sitting at the beginning of this second stage of Spiritual Evolution. I was actually surprised to see how mainstream it is becoming. Just today I saw one of America's leading presidential candidates declare himself to be a spiritual person, as opposed to using the usual political tactic of declaring oneself as being of the same religion as the majority of the land.

Because you are reading this book, I suspect that you are open to understanding the world and the divine through the lens of cultures other than what you were born into and have therefore evolved passed the closed-minded first stage and are probably situated in this more open, thoughtful, and mature second stage of Spiritual Evolution. I also however, suspect that perhaps you are ready to jump further ahead of the rest of society and progress to the third stage, if you are not there yet.

Contemplation

1. Observe your subtle body (mind, intelligence, and identity). How open are you to seeing the divine through multiple perspectives? Give yourself a score from 1 to 10, 10 being 100 percent open.

2. Observe that this second stage is becoming more and more society's norm. Keep your eyes out for public figures openly declaring an openness to other beliefs and faiths.

The 3rd Stage of Spiritual Evolution: Spiritual Wisdom in the Information Age

The weakness of the second stage of Spiritual Evolution is that in the endeavor to be respectful and inclusive, the spiritual path begins to lose its flavor and one's intelligent discernment is lost. Let me explain.

Loss of Flavor

Because the second stage of Spiritual Evolution is about inclusion and accepting those of different cultures and faiths, its' fully developed expression—spirituality—lacks any culture, tradition, or one-pointed faith. It becomes bland and loses the beauty, depth, and flavor that culture and tradition provide. Culture and ritual can help deepen a spiritual experience or understanding. In a sense, the second stage of Spiritual Evolution combines and homogenizes all of the unique special flavors that religious teachings provide and sees them all as one. By doing this, both the philosophical and cultural uniqueness of each faith are eradicated and thus everything becomes bland or even boring.

Have you ever visited a cathedral with large stained-glass windows and a choir singing their soul in prayer? Have you ever heard Islamic hymns echo from the top of a minaret? Have you ever felt the serenity of Buddhist monks in meditation? Have you ever marveled at the colorful latticework of song and dance in a Hindu ritual? All of these things have flavor, sweetness, depth, and dimension, and are designed to bring you deeper into your relationship with the Divine. By homogenizing them together or abolishing their uniqueness, their beauty is lost.

Being an Insider

The experience of being an outsider witnessing these spiritual practices and ceremonies cannot match up to the feelings invoked by the sincere individual fully immersed on that particular religious path. Modern spirituality dabbles lightly in some of this beauty but often loses the depth of connection available in a committed path and culture. Please do not misunderstand me: Spirituality is great, and certainly far more advanced than the closed-minded dogma of the first stage. Just as first-stage religion is perfect for some people, for where they are at in their spiritual evolution, spirituality may be just the perfect thing for other individuals to connect with the Divine. No two snowflakes are the same, no two spiritual journeys are the same, and we all have our own individual perfect path to follow. I know many people who have gone very, very deep in their spiritual evolution while staying in the first and second stages.

Choosing the 3rd Stage

I do, however, suggest that you enter the third stage of Spiritual Evolution and get the best of both worlds. Like in the second stage, people in the third stage are open to respecting and understanding other faiths. They see that because the Divine is unlimited there are also unlimited paths to reach and understand Him/Her/It. They love and respect everyone and everyone's path, and at the same time find that there is a special nectar, a special love, bliss, or joy in having a one-pointed relationship with the divine. They realize that the colorfulness of culture is not a merely outdated ritual made by the primitive people of the past, but that culture, traditions, and rituals have been used by all spiritual paths for thousands of years to deepen connection with the Divine. They find that spiritual traditions, rituals, practices, and stories are not only tools for connecting with the Divine, but they also provide deep insight into the very nature of the transcendental domain.

They know there is a certain dimension of connection that comes only by diving deeply into a path, and they thus choose to dive deep into one path. Yet they are not naïve: They know culture is always evolving and they know ultimately pure, passionate Spiritual Enlightenment is beyond all culture and tradition. In essence they love respect and learn from all paths, while at the same time dive deeply into one path. They have not fallen for the bland, homogenized shallowness of second-stage openness and though they are open to, accepting of, and respectful to all they have a preferred name that they would rather call God by.

The Blind Men and the Elephant

Once upon a time, three blind men came across an elephant. They had not heard of such a creature before so they began to touch it to learn what it was. One man said the elephant was a long pipe that blows air. Another man said the elephant was a sturdy, big, and round tree-like animal. The other man said the elephant was a thin rope with a tassel on the end.

Like spirituality and religion, all men were right; they were just seeing it from different angles.

Discrimination in the 3rd Stage

Another facet of the third stage is discrimination. In life we are always choosing, comparing, and evaluating. When we go shopping we compare prices and deals. When we buy something as simple as a banana we use our judgment and pick the better bunch. But in the fear of becoming a first-stage bigot, often times people in the second stage turn off their discerning mind and simply accept all spiritual paths as the same.

There is no other area in life in which such lack of evaluation would be acceptable. But for some reason when it comes to the spiritual path, which is the most important aspect of our life, a purely second-stage person will do no comparing or evaluating and just simply see all ideas as the same.

Just as every car at the dealership has its pros and cons, just as all universities are not created equal, and just as every potato grows differently, in the same way a third-stage individual understands that not all spiritual paths are the same, and they respectfully and carefully use both their head and heart to discern the better path. They are not self-indulged, prejudiced bigots like some people who are on the first stage; rather, they love, respect, and value all people and all spiritual paths. They just simply understand that their spiritual journey is extremely important and they want to find the best and most effective way of progressing to enlightenment.

Levels of Enlightenment and the 3rd Stage

People in the third stage understand that different people have different levels of desire. Some people want enlightenment and to know God more than others. They also know that everyone is on a different stage in their spiritual journey. Thus they understand that all different spiritual paths and religions exist to cater to people according to where they are in their spiritual journey and how much they really want to see, know, and experience the Divine.

The best and most relevant path for one person is not the best or most relevant for another. Each person has an individual nature—a personal dharma—and different spiritual paths resonate with different people. A third-stage spiritual practitioner knows which path resonates with them the most and has that path or faith as their central focus. Other paths may provide them with value, support, guidance, and inspiration, and they accept it with joy, yet they remain resolute in their path and their relationship with the Divine.

They may also find that some parts of the culture, tradition, teachings, or mindsets that are associated with their chosen path do not resonate or support them and thus they choose not to accept those unhelpful parts. I am known as the Maverick Monk because there are elements of the monk culture that I feel don't currently serve me in advancing to Passionate Enlightenment. The truth is, we are all responsible for our own spiritual journey, and we need to follow and accept only those teaching and practices that work for us. In a sense a third-stage spiritual practitioner carves out their own spiritual path.

Exercise

1. Seek the beauty in other cultures and paths. Practice not judging others and finding the beauty and power in their way of relating with the Divine.

2. Learn about various spiritual paths and challenge the spiritual ideas you grew up with. Just because you were born in a culture or religion does not mean it is the most

helpful for you. If you are going to truly advance to the highest and deepest levels of enlightenment, you need to consciously choose your own spiritual path.

3. When learning from a teacher, try to observe which of the three stages they are coming from. Naturally I recommend learning from those strongly fixed in the third stage.

CHAPTER 15

THE 3 STAGES OF ENLIGHTENMENT AND THE DIVINE

You are well on your path to understanding and tasting the magnificent splendor of the Divine. In order to act in the most effective way possible and in order to fully manifest your greatest spiritual potential, we shall now learn the three stages of Enlightenment, which can also be called the three understandings of the Divine.

I have observed that all religions and spiritual paths fall into at least one of these three categories, or understandings, of the Divine, and I find that if you just understand these three ways of viewing the Divine, then you can clearly see where every spiritual idea or religious doctrine fits. Then you can make a wise and informed decision about what kind of spiritual journey you want.

> We all connect with the same truth in different ways. Just like the sun is called different names in different languages and even shines with different intensities in different places, there are many names, relationships, and approaches to understanding the same energy or person, that I have been calling the Divine and many call God.

The One Indivisible, Absolute Divine Spiritual Truth as Three?

The majority of the 5,000-year-old wisdom texts of India known as Veda were compiled by an enlightened sage named Vyas. The reason why it is said that this wisdom was *compiled*, rather than *authored*, is because, as previously described, true knowledge is an eternal principle accessible to anyone spiritually surrendered enough to tune into it. Legend has it that Vyas needed a scribe to write down the poetry-like hymns of the Vedas that he would compose and dictate. Another great being, known as Ganesha, volunteered to write down these verses as long as Vyas's dictation was such that the scribe's pen would not stop moving. Once the scribe's pen stopped, he would write no more.

The wisdom of the Vedas is a complex explanation of everything in existence and it is composed in poetry. It is hard to expect someone, even an enlightened sage like Vyas, to instantly tune into and compile such wisdom with elegance and cohesion. Vyas in turn agreed to the conditions of the scribe on the condition that the scribe understood everything that he wrote.

In the beginning of the dictation, Vyas spoke one verse that encapsulated all the knowledge of the Divine. Due to the vast nature of the Divine this verse was complex and had many layers of depth to it. Therefore, in the time that it took the scribe to comprehend it, Vyas was able to mentally compose the rest of the verses of the Vedas.

This complex Sanskrit verse in essence says that all of the extremely intelligent intellectuals and enlightened people of the past have understood the same one indivisible, supreme absolute reality in three different ways. These three completely different ways of understanding God or the

Divine are all correct, yet they seem contradictory. How can something that is one and indivisible be three?

Stage 1: Preliminary Understanding of the Divine: Braman (Technically Brahman or Brahma)

The first understanding of the non-dual indivisible one supreme absolute reality is an impersonal one. This concept says that there is a transcendental Divine supreme energy that exists everywhere, that all things exist within this energy, and that this energy is within all things. This energy is like a kind of spiritual effulgent white light and people connect with it through meditation and other spiritual practices.

When you progress in this understanding, you can see that all things are merely a transformation of this energy. All the eight elements are this energy and every car, house, animal, or plant is also just a part of this energy. With this preliminary understanding of the Divine you begin to see that actually all things are one. You will find that difference and separation between things are an illusion and that the feeling of separation between people and things is what causes all pain and suffering.

In this preliminary understanding of the Divine, enlightenment is when peace and the destruction of suffering are attained through complete absorption in the spiritual "white light." When fully absorbed, the practitioner gives up their individual identity and thus almost merges into this light that is known as Braman in the Sanskrit language. Because everything and everyone is Braman, you can say that those who have attained this type of enlightenment have merged into the totality of life.

In this stage of enlightenment one's identification with the subtle and physical bodies is destroyed, plus their individual identity of the soul is hidden.

Thus all suffering is destroyed. There is no possibility of pain because there is no one to feel the pain. The joy of being 100-percent pain-free is naturally fabulous, and thus full absorption in Braman is a source of immense joy. This joy of being 100-percent absorbed in Braman is the joy of just being you; the soul without any material identification with the physical and subtle bodies is far greater than any joy available through trying to enjoy in this world. No pleasure derived from any of your senses or mind such as any food, smell, or orgasm can come close to the pleasure of connecting with and being absorbed in this divine, transcendental "white light," Braman.

When one is fully absorbed in Braman, they feel no suffering or pain, they are always happy, the troubles and tribulations of this world no longer bother them, and they remain equipoised, balanced, and peaceful in every situation, for they are detached and absorbed in transcendence. They see all things as equal and make no differentiation among a dog, a cow, a human, or a plant, for they see everything simply as a transformation of Braman.

In my travels many people have approached me in confidence asking me to explain a spiritual experience they have had. Oftentimes there was a split-second in meditation where they actually got a glimpse of Braman. They tell me that they have never felt anything like it and have spent years trying figure out what happened to them and how they can get that feeling again.

Fully absorbing oneself into this "white light" is the goal and objective of many spiritual seekers and religions. I believe that most of Buddhism is trying to attain this state of full absorption; they call it nirvana. I find that there are even some people in the religions that believe a personal God-like Christianity, Judaism, and Islam that don't really see God as a person in the same way that their religions teach; they see God more as an all-pervading energy. There is even a section of Hinduism that only aspires for *mukti*, or liberation from suffering, which is basically this preliminary understanding of the Divine. I have noticed that the culmination of most modern spirituality also is to lead to this Braman realization.

This concept of Braman is the concept that you will arrive at if you try to understand God or the divine by your own power, logic, and intellect. It is only by surrendering spiritually and receiving loving support from beyond this Braman stage that one can progress beyond this concept.

Being fully absorbed in Braman, being completely pain-free, always being situated in transcendence, being fully detached from all things of this world, and always feeling inner contentment, and thus being enlightened (in the preliminary understanding of the Divine) is no simple feat. It can take many lifetimes to come to such a stage. Like I said, entire religions are steeped in this concept, and some of the most intelligent people in history have spent their entire lives searching and intellectualizing to finally reach this state. There are entire books on this concept and many practices on how to attain this state of Braman.

Given the vastness of this subject there is so much more I could write, but we must move on and learn the next two sweeter understandings of the one indivisible absolute truth. But before we do so, here is a small metaphoric story to help you comprehend these highly complex and extremely deep concepts.

Story of the Villagers and the Train (Part One)

A few hundred years ago, there was a village. This village was remote and very primitive, and they had no electricity. They had little-to-no contact with any of the progress of modern society, yet they heard tales of a magnificent invention called a train. No one really knew what this train thing was, so there were many speculations and ideas going around about what it might be.

Finally, one boy had enough. He was going to figure this train thing out once and for all, so he decided to walk to the train tracks that were some miles away from the village. It took him eight hours to walk there, and when he arrived it was night. Then suddenly he saw a huge light in the distance speeding toward him. He had never seen such a big light at night. He knew for sure that he had finally seen it: He had seen a train; he finally knew what this legendary thing was.

As his heart filled with excitement and his body with adrenaline, he ran back to the village. All the villagers gathered around him as he declared what a train was. He said that a train is a huge bright light that shines at night. The light rushes toward you and is brighter than anything you have seen or will ever see.

This explanation satisfied the villages for some days, until more questions began to surface, including "What does a train look like in the daytime?" To be continued. . .

———

This metaphor is akin to people trying to understand the one supreme indivisible absolute truth or God and coming to the Preliminary Understanding of the Divine. Yes, it is true that a train is a big light that moves speedily toward you at night; and yes, it is true that the Divine is an all-pervading divine energy that you can absorb yourself into and practically dissolve your individual identity into it. The Divine does end suffering and inspire inner peace, but there is so much more.

> **Contemplation:** Think of at least three concepts or ideas that you have heard or read that may fall into the category of this preliminary understanding of the Divine. Here are a few examples:
>
> - "We are all one."
> - "Separation is an Illusion."
> - "You are that."

Stage 2: Abridged Understanding of the Divine: Paramatama

This next concept of the Divine builds on the first. A spiritual seeker will generally evolve from the first to the second to the third understanding of the Divine. But such sequential progression is not necessary, and you may go directly to any understanding.

The Supersoul

After some time of witnessing the effulgent bright light of Braman, you may be fortunate enough to see that this light does not just live as light: Beyond it there is a being. There is a silhouette of a person. Beyond the oneness there is a diversity. Upon seeing Him/Her you may not yet have full knowledge of who this being is, but there is being nonetheless.

The amazing light of Braman, which many spiritualists spend their entire life trying to catch a glimpse of or merge with, is simply the bright effulgence that emanates from the body of this elusive Being. This Being is known as the Paramatama or the Supersoul.

Present Everywhere

Paramatama is present everywhere. He (I am calling Him a He for now; in the next chapter we will explore the masculine and feminine aspects of the divine) exists inside of everything and outside of everything; He is near and He is far. He is in every atom of the Universe and the Universe exists within Him. All of existence manifests from Him, and he pervades every inch, millimeter, and atom of it.

The best part of this all is He lives in your heart. He watches everything you do and does not judge. He simply advises, waits for your love, and supplies the results of your actions.

The ancient wisdom of India says that we do our duty, our dharma, and the results of such actions are provided by God. We may plant a seed but it is the Divine that causes it to grow. The expression of God that does the actual growing is this Paramatma; He exists within the seed and inspires it to grow. It is said that not a blade of grass moves without the permission of the Divine. The all-pervading Divine that knows everything and gives permission for all things to move and be is this Paramatma or Supersoul. He is the doer, witness, and support of all things.

Two Birds in a Tree

The 5,000-year-old Vedic texts give the example of two birds sitting in a tree. One is eating the fruits and the other is watching. The bird that is watching is waiting for the bird that is eating to turn and connect in love.

In this metaphor, the tree is the body, the fruit-eating bird is you, and the soul, that is acting in this world eating the fruits of your actions and the other bird, is this Supersoul, who is watching and waiting and thinking, "When will my beloved turn and look at me? I am here to help, guide, and love."

Individuality Is Kept

When you advance to this abridged understanding of the Divine, your individuality is maintained. You don't dissolve your identity and lose your sense of self like when you realize Braman. You maintain a sense of duality with this understanding. On one hand you experience as you are the individual soul, and on the other hand you experience the Divine as Paramatma.

A key motive for those seeking to merge with Braman is to end suffering. Suffering comes from separation and therefore the Braman seeking faiths strive to merge and thus end the distance and separation that cause all the pain. Those who approach spiritual growth on the level of Paramatma see Him everywhere, and relate and connect with Him through all things. When they are walking they see the ground as Paramatma, when they breathe they see the air as Paramatma, and when they are in trouble they call out and pray to Paramatma, who is always there to support. In this understanding of the Divine, the realizations and goals of those on the Braman stage are attained and included. Suffering is destroyed because there is always a unity with the all-pervading Paramatma, and thus no merging is required.

From this duality of both you and the Divine being separate individuals a fantastic love play is born. This love affair reaches its most succulent ripeness in the highest and final understanding of the Divine that is coming up—after we learn a little more about Paramatama.

Inner Intuition

Have you ever felt something inside of you guiding you? Some people call this guidance "intuition." This is not just the innate knowledge of the soul that we learned in Chapter 13 but a higher guidance that comes from the Divine. Such inner guidance comes from the Paramatma, and therefore the Paramatma is often called the inner Guru.

An external Guru—that exists in flesh and blood—is considered an expansion of this inner Guru because He/She is in a permanent love bond with Paramatma and thus can guide you according to Paramatma's instructions. A Guru is vital for rapid spiritual growth for so many reasons, one of them being because we often are quite deaf to the inner guidance of Paramatma, and therefore the guidance of an external Guru is needed.

In essence, you can say that Spiritual Surrender is about learning how to tune in and follow the guidance of the Divine. Such guidance is given by Paramatma.

Remember that any internal guidance from the Divine must be perfect. Because He is everywhere, knows everything, and has your best interest in mind, He will guide you to the best possible action. Therefore the most effective action is not a result of identity, intelligence, or even desire. It is that action that is guided by the Divine. Such magnificent surrender is your Eternal Dharma.

At the time I am writing this book, the idea of "the Universe" as something that guides, supports, and supplies the fruits of your actions or wishes is a popular one. This idea and relationship with the Universe is a relationship with Paramatma.

One of the main distinctions of knowing the Divine as Paramatma as opposed to any other understanding is that, though a relationship exists, we are not quite sure who or what this Paramatma person is. We know He exists and some of what He does, but the full details of who this Being is, is only available in the next unabridged Bhagavan understanding of the Divine.

When people relate with "the Universe," it is not always clear exactly what that is, yet still their experience and connection are real. I know many successful millionaires who operate and make important choices according to what they "feel from the Universe." I used to think this to be airy-fairy, but I can't deny their success, and now that I know that it is Paramatma they are relating with, it all makes sense.

Paramatma and Yoga

People know yoga is not simply an exercise system, it is a spiritual system. The very word *yoga* mean to link or unite. The true purpose of yoga is to realize and unite with the Paramatma Supersoul. The exercises are merely tools to pacify and balance the eight elements in your body so that you can enter a meditative state to connect with Paramatma. Yoga poses can also be used as tools to tune into the guidance of Paramatma. This subject of yoga is a large one, and there is so much insight to it that is not yet present in the Western world.

Paramatma and Prayer

Whenever a spiritual path or religion refers to God in your heart, inner guidance, a sign from God, praying, God existing everywhere, or God watching you, whether they know this system or terminology they are referring to the Paramatma or Supersoul understanding of the Divine.

> **Contemplation:** Think of at least three times when you felt connected to the Divine. A time when you felt that something or someone was there and you were not alone, you may have not been quite sure who or what it was, but you surely felt a spiritual accompaniment of some sort. This is the Paramatma or Supersoul.

Exercise

The next time you feel an inner calling or inner guidance, follow it—even if you don't understand it and the instructions don't make sense to you at the time.

The Story of the Villagers and the Train (Part Two)

A second boy in the village decided he was going to get a better understanding of what a train was by seeing it in the daytime. He set off and when he arrived at the tracks, he saw the huge shining light in the distance rushing toward him like the first boy had described. But he also saw a big house on wheels with a smoke-spitting chimney that was charging faster than anything he had ever seen. It was amazing! He, too, was filled with excitement and ran back to the village to tell everyone of his findings. He concluded that a train was both a white light and a house on wheels.

This part of the story exemplifies the understanding of Paramatma; Now things are more concrete and clear. Through the light, shape is beginning to form, the villagers are getting a clearer understanding of a train, and we are getting a clearer understanding of the Divine. We are beginning to see what or who the "Spirit" is in "spiritual."

CHAPTER 16

A LOVING RELATIONSHIP WITH THE DIVINE

My friend, now we get to the most fun, sweetest, and most heartwarmingly beautiful understanding of the Divine: the concept of Bhagavan.

We have come a long way together. In Part 1 we learned crucial foundational principles for any complete knowledge system, such as the integration of the spiritual and material and the principle of dharma. In Part 2, we learned the nature of the world and how to be effective in it by using the Unprecedented Elemental Reality System. And in this last and most important section we are learning the very nature of the Divine and what it means for us in our life.

The Story of a Hollywood Dance

Some years ago, a friend of mine invited me to come see her perform in a fancy Hollywood dance production. Spiritually themed, and depicting the story of someone striving on the path of enlightenment, they acted out his many troubles along the way, showing how sometimes the influences and temptations of this world can derail the spiritual seeker.

What I found intriguing was that every time they showed the temptations of this world the dance was elegant and detailed, the music was extraordinary, and the whole thing was just a magnificently beautiful spectacle. On the other hand, when they depicted Enlightenment it was all quite bland: someone meditating with a spotlight shining on him, accompanied by simpler music.

I tried to understand why the depiction of what was supposed to be negative and temporary temptation had so much more splendor than their depiction of enlightenment.

I came to two conclusions:

1. The choreographers did not know much about the Divine or Enlightenment. They had lots of information about the temptations of this world, so they were able to compose an exquisite spectacle about it, but their knowledge of the Divine was limited. I think the same goes for most people. Most people don't really have a detailed idea of the Divine realm, because it is something that is outside of most people's experience and reality. Just like in life, it is helpful to know about what you are trying to achieve. It is also important that we have a solid understanding of Enlightenment if we are serious about attaining it.

2. Reverse anthropomorphization. I know, that's a long, fancy term. Basically anthropomorphism is when someone applies human attributes onto God. They may think because they have two arms and two legs God must also have two arms and two legs, for example. What my somewhat-comical term *reverse anthropomorphization* means is that when someone thinks that because man or the world is one way, then the spiritual domain or God must be the complete opposite. They falsely think that if there is color, flavor, sex, fun, and diversity here in this world, then the spiritual domain must not have these things and therefore must be boring and bland.

Though there is some truth to this tranquil and docile concept of enlightenment—it is the preliminary understanding of the Divine—the fact remains that the highest form of enlightenment is passionate and full of more color, flavor, and vigor than is possible in this world.

The Unprecedented Elemental Reality System shows us how the physical is a condensation and expression of the subtle. What exists in our physical reality is the result of our subtle reality. The domain of the divine is the most subtle, so we can logically conclude that what exists in physical reality also exists in the divine.

Because there is so much beauty, sweetness, and flavor in this world, the Divine must be filled with even greater amounts of such beauty, joy, flavor, and dimension because what exists in creation also exists in its creator.

Another thing that I became aware of through watching this Hollywood dance is that there is such a gross misrepresentation of the spiritual path and enlightenment in society. Why would anyone want to follow a spiritual path, if it was as it is commonly depicted? Imagine if enlightenment was just a bland negation of suffering mixed with some peacefulness? Enlightenment is wrongly depicted more like a drowsy retirement home than the musical dancing escapade it is. The spiritual bliss of enlightenment is the ultimate thrill!

To be fair, the bland, simplistic form of enlightenment that many people hold in their minds is a distant observation of the preliminary understanding of the Divine, so it does have some validity.

Unabridged Understanding of the Divine: Bhagavan

You can pronounce this as Bagavan or Bagawan.

Once the spiritual practitioner has destroyed suffering with the preliminary understanding of the Divine, after She/He is under the guidance of and connected to Paramatma, She/He can now begin to passionately connect with the Divine in the most complete and playful way.

Evolving From Paramatma to Bhagavan

One who knows the Supersoul knows that God is with them at all times. Such a person connects with Paramatma regularly; they follow His guidance, ask for answers, and regularly bask in the meditative serenity of His divine company. If they are ever in trouble they simply look into their heart and seek the counsel and support of the all-pervading and all-knowing Paramatma, and thus their relationship with Him continues to thicken and deepen.

In time they wonder: Who is this Divine being that I am always connecting with? They are in a type of communication with Paramatma and therefore know that He is a person and they wonder: What is His/Her Name? What are His/Her likes and dislikes? Where is He/She from? How does He/She look? What does He/She do?

In search for answers to these questions the sincere spiritual practitioner comes to the third and final Unabridged Bhagavan Understanding of the Divine.

Bhagavan

The third and final unabridged Bhagavan understanding of the Divine says that the highest and most complete understanding of the Divine is to see God as a person. The concept of Bhagavan says that the person who is God has likes, dislikes, friends, family, lovers, thoughts, and feelings, and all the faculties that any person would. This understanding seeks above all to know God, the person.

The Bhagavan concept agrees with both the preliminary and abridged understandings of the Divine, it just takes things one step further.

God As a Person?

First-stage dogmatic religion, as described in Chapter 14, will fight to establish that the person they view God to be is the one and only. People have been mercilessly killed for not accepting a certain view of who or what God is. Therefore in modern times it is politically safe to gently avoid the subject of God as a person. But, my friend, this does not mean that the discussion should not be had, nor that the discussion has to be painful or disrespectful in any way. There is a beautiful reconciliation that allows almost all beliefs about the divine to coexist in a relaxing harmony.

Avatar

The Vedas teach that the dharma of the Divine is to taste every type of happiness, love relationship, and flavor there is to taste. By definition God is unlimited and therefore has the ability to manifest an individual and unique form that is perfectly suited and ideal for tasting each relationship and each type of happiness in existence. This is not saying that there are many Gods but that there is one God that takes on many forms or avatars.

This is actually not such a far-fetched idea when you think of it; we all do this in some capacity. Take a high court judge, for example. When he is at work he wears a certain uniform, he has a different name (Your Honor), and people see and treat him differently (with reverence). When relating with his children he has a different role, has a different name (Daddy), wears a different style dress, and is seen and treated differently. When he is on a date with his wife, his name is now Honey, he dresses differently, and he has a different function and role. For each relationship and situation he has a different avatar. He, in a sense, is a different person in each situation.

In the same way the 5,000-year-old spiritual wisdom of Veda says that God does the same thing, just on a grander scale. Some religions relate with God in one of His avatars or expansions, and others relate with a different avatar of God. Each of the relationships with God and their accompanying names, practices, and rituals are valid, are real, and most importantly do not cancel out any other relationships.

The word *avatar* is a Sanskrit word that specifically conveys the topic of God's multiple expansions. I find it inspiring to see how words such as *avatar, yoga, karma, dharma, guru,* and so forth have entered the Western vocabulary. Sometimes the meanings and absolutely profound concepts related to these words are distorted; that's why I make videos and write articles about these concepts on *www.themaverickmonk.com/blog*

The Story of the Villagers and the Train (Part Three)

After some time, some of the villagers began to think: Why was there a big house on wheels with a chimney and big lights moving so fast along the track? Who was driving the train? What was in the train? Who lived in this mysterious house on wheels?

Eager to know the whole truth, another villager followed the tracks to the train station. He saw people getting on and off the train, and he met the train driver, the passengers, and the station master.

He now knew the people behind the train and why they used the train. This villager actually knew the train in its entirety. He saw the light and saw the house on wheels, but real knowledge came when he met the people behind it.

In the same way, the most enlightened being is the one who understands all three aspects of the Divine and relates with Him or Her in this Bhagavan understanding of the Divine through passionately enlightened love.

> **Contemplation:** Think about whether you prefer to interact with a real person when you shop or call customer service. Do you prefer to do business with nameless, faceless, and bland corporation? Chances are you want to deal with a person. Corporations know this and spend millions to humanize themselves. I see that this need for personal interaction is a reflection of the soul's need to connect. The soul is always yearning to fulfill its highest dharma by connecting personally. Our heart cries for an eternal loving connection with a God who has a name, who forms qualities, and who has pastimes. The soul cannot be fully satisfied only interacting with an impersonal, nameless, and formless energy.

Love, Love, Love and the Divine

Throughout this book I have repeatedly referred to a special type of love—a love and connection with the Divine that is out of this world. I have mentioned how this love is our Eternal Dharma and therefore an inseparable part of the soul. I mentioned how acting in this spiritual love and surrender is the most powerful and satisfying thing you can do, but what I have not yet done is given you a detailed and complete understanding of this love and how to get it. The whole point, not just this book but every one of my trainings, is to empower you to live and taste this highest and sweetest love. Everything you have read in this book thus far has simply been a foundation so that we can enter into this subject of pure, selfless spiritual love.

In order to understand the gravity of such love we will explore the beginning and foundation of existence from the Vedic perspective. Some people consider this metaphor and others consider it fact. Whichever version you choose works and will enable you to access this immense cosmic love of the Divine.

The Indivisible One Becomes Two

The wisdom of Veda says that originally everything was one: There were no planets, galaxies, skies, starts, stones, animals, or people; God and His creation were all united together as one Being.

Now, there is no fun in being nothing and doing nothing; there is no pleasure in being a homogeneous void. Therefore, that Supreme Being, the Indivisible One Supreme Absolute Truth, that all-pervading and all-powerful Being that many call God, made the cosmic decision to have fun. He, She, or It wanted to enjoy, feel pleasure, and share love.

I am telling this story as if it were history because the English language requires me to. In actuality, this all "happened" outside of the construct of time and space, so there is no past, present, or future in this story.

In order to share love, the Divine divided Himself in two because you cannot enjoy, share love, or have a good party alone, and God, being the source of all knowledge, knows this best.

When God divided Himself, one form was masculine and the other form was feminine. Each had a role to play in this divine dance, so each side held certain functions. The feminine was the power, energy, and executor; the masculine was the powerful, the energetic, and the desirer.

These two facets of God were and are divine lovers. The ancient Vedic traditions say the original name of the feminine aspect of the divine is Radha, which means one whose being is completely composed of and permeated by passionate loving affection. The name of the masculine is Krishna, which literally means the all-attractive being that will draw you in with piercing beauty and satisfy you fully. There are many names for these two throughout the Vedic literature and throughout the world's many languages, religions, and cultures. I like the names Radha and Krishna because they are imbued with love, relationships, and sweetness, so from here on I will use the name Krishna to refer to the masculine aspect of God and Radha for the feminine.

Unlimited Desire

By nature, the Supreme Being (God) is unlimited. Therefore among other things the masculine aspect of the Divine, Krishna, has unlimited ever increasing desires. The feminine aspect of the Divine, Radha, is the executor and the personification of power. She thus is unlimitedly powerful. She uses Her unlimited power to manifest and create everything in existence solely to satisfy the unlimited desires of Her beloved Krishna. Every planet, galaxy, tree, sky, and waterfall have been created by Radha simply to satisfy, please, and pleasure Krishna, and to facilitate their eternal love affair.

Radha and Krishna

Once upon a time Krishna, a beautiful boy, was sitting under a tree. He was sad and lonely. The desire to enjoy and connect in love swelled in His heart and from the left half of His body a divine Goddess appeared. She was bedecked in exquisite jewels, wore a flower garland, and looked as if she was beauty personified. Her heart was filled with intense passionate love for Krishna, and She began to run toward Him.

Contemplation: Some cultures stress the masculine aspect of the divine; other cultures, the feminine. Think of the culture you grew up in. Did it prefer seeing the Divine as a masculine God, or as a feminine Goddess?

Everything Is Created From Love

The main point of the story of Radha and Krishna is that love and creation are intertwined. Love is the source, the origin, and the cause for all things to exist. When you look out into nature and into how things happen in the world, you will also find that love, whether it is in the form of sex, cross-pollination, or communication, is what creates and grows things. There is a lot more to this concept of the interconnection of love and creation.

The story of Radha and Krishna teaches us that love permeates every atom and every cell of existence. Things only exist because of love and therefore they are made of love. The dharma of everything and everyone is to connect in love. All destruction, suffering, pain, and trauma are symptoms of a lack of love. Therefore my beloved Guru used to say, "God is love and Love is God."

If you want to be effective, powerful, and happy, connect in love. If you want money, success, or fame, connect in love. If you want peace, harmony, and unity, connect in love. Most importantly, if you want enlightenment, spiritual growth, and to know God, connect in love. Love is the be all and end all of all of existence. God is thirsty for love, we are thirsty for love, we are made of love, and love is our Eternal Dharma.

Quick Tip: All Power Lies in Connection

When looking to be effective or looking to gain more power in any area such as business, education, or relationships, the secret trick to is to increase connection. Love is a connection, and where there is no connection there is no power.

In business, love and connection take the form of communication, empathy, inspiration, goodwill, and so forth. If you increase the communication and connection between people within your company, productivity will increase. If you increase the communication and connection between the company and its customers, profits will rise. If you increase the communication and connection in your creative team, more will be created. For a business to create and grow rapidly there must be love, both within the company and between the company and its customers. If there is no love the company will die.

In education if you increase the communication and connection and positive feelings between the teacher and the student, the student will learn more. That is why the Eastern traditions promote a strong personal bond between Guru and disciple. This is also why I connect with my students in multiple ways, such as through my books, web classes, articles, live events, and retreats.

Love is more than just a connection. Care and affection are other key ingredients to love. Infuse your communication and connection with care and affection and you will not only be happier, you will also be more effective.

What do we value most? If you look at it, interacting with other people or animals is the most satisfying part of people's lives. We are social beings and what we do to get the love, approval, and acceptance of other living beings is mind-boggling. If you observe people, almost everything they do is about connecting with others. People get married, join clubs, watch TV, wear certain clothes, go to war, and so much more all out of the need to connect.

The Deeper Meaning of Om

The mantra word *om* (or *aum*) has become quite famous. When people think of meditating instinctively they begin to chant *om*. People know it's the meditation mantra, but few people know it's true deep meaning. In fact the word *om* is considered a seed mantra because it encapsulates all the knowledge of the Vedas. Every verse of the Vedas starts with *om*, and all the Vedic texts are simply an explanation and a commentary of this word. There are many levels of understandings of what *om* means. Some say *om* is the sound vibration that the Universe makes, but its meaning is much deeper.

In the Sanskrit language the word *om* is composed of three letters: A, U, and M. The A represents Krishna, or the masculine aspect of the supreme; the U represents Radha, or the feminine part of God; and the M represents you, or the individual living entity. In Sanskrit the A and the U conjunct together to create one letter signifying the transcendental lover and beloved, Radha and Krishna, God and His girlfriend, united together in a trans-mundane embrace. Radha and Krishna's love is not just for them; you are a part of this cosmic love affair, and the M signifies that. The M is you, the soul partaking in the dynamic dancing love play of the Divine.

In the Vedic tradition the mantra *om* is generally practiced when it appears as the first word of secret mantras that are given from Guru to disciple at the time of initiation or as part of the ritualistic and rhythmic chanting of the Vedic texts. The practice of chanting by itself is widespread and is pretty much done at the end of every yoga class. The next time you are chanting *om* you can now contemplate this deeper meaning. I suggest when chanting it you feel it as a calling to the Divine to connect in love and unite together with Radha and Krishna in their transcendental love play.

If you are looking for a daily meditation practice, which I highly recommend, the best practice I suggest is the Japa Mantra Meditation Practice (in Chapters 8 and 17). Also, watch the meditation video I made for you in your bonus section: eternaldharmabook.com/bonus

CHAPTER 17

How to Grow Spiritual Love

We briefly explored how everything originates from love, is made of love, and is made for love. Therefore we know that we simply need to increase love to increase the effectiveness of our actions and to progress to Passionate Enlightenment. But how do we do that?

The Need for Individuality in Love

First we must know that for love to exist there must be a giver and receiver. It takes two to tango, and it takes two exchanging energies and emotions for love to reach its highest form.

This may seem obvious, but this fact is often overlooked by the spiritual seekers who look through the eyes of the impersonal preliminary understanding of the Divine, which denies duality.

Beyond Worldly Love

Before we dive into the process of growing and developing this love, please know that not all love is created equal: Love comes in different intensities. We may be head over heels in love with our boyfriend, girlfriend, spouse, or children, but just be moderately in love with our neighbors, friends, and acquaintances. This is natural.

The sad truth of life is that the love of this world, whether for family, friends, and lovers, is most probably infected with the selfishness of God Syndrome and therefore not pure. We identify with our physical and subtle bodies, and we can only love other physical and subtle bodies, and therefore cannot fully love at all. You can only fully love on a soul level if you fully know who you are as a soul. Therefore if you are not fully enlightened, your love will be based on the body, and this bodily based love is love of a much, much, much smaller intensity than the full-fledged love of Passionate Enlightenment.

The purest, highest love is love for the Divine. The dharma of the soul, above all things, is to primarily love God. This concept is often misunderstood by spiritual practitioners who sometimes think that to primarily love God means we are not supposed to love our fellow human beings. Though a love based on the body is inherently faulty, we still must love other living beings if we are to be happy and to love God. A soft heart that is affectionate to all is one of the qualities of an advanced spiritualist.

The difference between loving people when enlightened and the faulty love of this world is that enlightened love is not an isolated action; the Divine is part of the equation. First we love God, and through the Divine we powerfully love and connect to all living beings. This is the way of enlightened love.

My friend, when we are not fully enlightened, the ability of the soul to love is not fully developed. It is like a seed: There is something there, but it is not fully mature yet. The fully grown tree of love of God in Enlightenment is where the real power and joy are.

The Goal and the Process Are the Same

To grow the tree of fully enlightened spiritual love of the Divine, you must know that both the process and the end goal are the same. The goal is love, and therefore the process to attain that goal is also love.

We have some love in us now and as we offer it onto the Divine that love increases. Then with that increased amount of love we can offer more love, which in turn increases our love, enabling us to offer more. This process continues until we are fully Passionately Enlightened.

Another way to view this is if you see loving the Divine as water, every time you offer love you are pouring water on your sprouting seed of spiritual love. Needless to say, serving with fully mature love is your Eternal Dharma.

> **Contemplation:** Think of the sweetest relationship you have ever had or heard of. Remember how it made or makes you feel; remember the joy and the pain and how your heart melted. Now imagine the intensity, sweetness, and beauty of that relationship multiplied by infinity. Such joy is but a shadow of the relationship you can have in this full and complete unabridged Bhagavan understanding of the Divine. Such a relationship is your Eternal Dharma.

What Is Love?

When speaking so much about love it is important to define what we are speaking about. Love takes on many shapes and forms, and exists in many levels of intensity. Again, this is a subject for an entire book or training program, but in simplified essence, I see love as both an energy and a giving of energy. Every time we give energy, we are giving a bit of love.

Love and the Elements and Spiritual Surrender

I taught about the elements in Part 2 of this book so that you can see energy in its various forms. According to the Vedas all the elements are a transformation of the same energy. To be exact they are different iteration of the feminine aspect of the divine, Radha. Radha is love and Radha is energy.

To love the Divine, simply offer, give, and surrender both your heart and soul, and the elements on to Him. As a soul you have the power to control a certain amount of energy, so to advance spiritually, offer as much of your energy to the Divine as you can.

There are multitudes of spiritual practices in both the Vedas and in the thousands of spiritual faiths around the world. All of these practices basically boil down to the same thing: giving energy to the divine in one way or another.

How to Use Each of the Elements to Advance Spiritually

Following are some specific ways that are prescribed in the Vedas in which you can use each of the elements to advance in spiritual love. Of course, there are unlimited ways to serve, love, and engage in a spiritual love play with the Divine, and you can use your creativity and follow the direction of Paramatma (or Guru) to uncover them. All forms of loving service are most effective when imbued with the beauty of Spiritual Surrender.

When choosing how to serve, keep in mind what we learned in Part 2 of this book: There is more energy in the subtle than there is in the physical, and the subtle is more powerful and more important than the physical. Therefore it is best to use the more subtle elements in the service of God. This does not negate using the physical ones; in fact the best and ideal way to love and serve is to use all the elements plus the desire of the soul in the service of Divine.

Earth, Water, and Fire

In this context I am categorizing earth, water, and fire together to mean physical things.

1. Offer everything you eat to the Divine before you eat. Many religions and traditions do this. A simple Vedic mantra and process

to do this is, before eating sprinkle a little water on the food to purify it first; and chant the mantra "Sri Vishnu Sri Vishnu Sri Vishnu" and mentally visualize offering the food to the Divine. A common and more fancy way that people do this in India is to place the food on an altar in front of a deity or picture of a deity (you can use the image of Radha and Krishna) and ring a bell while saying "Sri Vishnu Sri Vishnu Sri Vishnu" at least once.

2.   Do the Offering Up Exercise: Before any action, take a moment to mentally offer that action to the divine. You can say, "Oh my beloved Lord, I offer this action on to you." Another version of this exercise is to offer all your physical objects to the Divine. Simply touch any physical object and say with love in your heart, "Oh my Beloved Krishna (or whatever name resonates with you), I offer this object onto you. It is yours now and I shall use it in your service."

3.   Build structures such as temples, churches, and businesses for the service of the Divine

Air

Air is prana/energy/chi. The true Ashtanga yoga process is to enter into a deep meditation and control the air element in your body. A powerful yogi then takes this energy and offers it unto Paramatma in his or her heart. This is a hard and complicated process; a super simple version would be to offer that good, buzz-like feeling of energy you feel during a yoga exercise on to the Divine.

You can also use the concept of air as raw energy, supplying churches, temples, monks, priests, and so forth with food, money, and the other materials needed to fuel their operations. Many religions do this by tithing. I have a list of spiritual projects that I sponsor and support, and it not only brings my heart solace to do so, I also feel love increasing.

Ether

Ether, being the midway point between the physical and the subtle, is one of the most important focal points for your spiritual advancement.

The best way to use ether is in Mantra Meditation. If there was only one thing that I would have you do after reading this book it would be Mantra Meditation. It is just the best processes for so many reasons.

When doing Mantra Meditation focus on offering your words in love to the Divine, try to give more of your heart with each word, and your love will gradually increase to propelling you into new realms of sweetness. The more you surrender in your mantra chanting, the more powerful it becomes.

Mantra Meditation (Japa): The Most Important Practice of This Book

Mantra Meditation is actually quite a simple practice. Basically what you do is repeat a mantra over and over again. This can be done at any time and in any place. A more formal and structured practice will yield greater results, though, so I will describe how to do such a practice here.

Note: The most common and best way to practice mantra chanting is to have a pre-set number of times to chant the mantra before you start the meditation. The auspicious number according to the 5,000-year-old tradition of India is 108 times. To count without having your mind distracted by the numbers, it's best to get a bead set with 108 beads.

1. Set some time aside and pick a quiet, clean, and peaceful place. Remove any possible distractions, like your cell phone, and sit down.
2. Hold the beads with your thumb and middle figure while having your index finger pointing out. If you do not have beads than you may use a clicker, or timer for you mantra mediation practice.
3. On each bead chant the mantra once, then move to the next bead. Once you have done one 108-bead cycle, you have completed one "round." You can start with one round a day and then gradually increase the number of rounds. About 16 rounds are ideal. In the beginning one round could take you up to 25 minutes, but when you are in practice and are chanting a lot of rounds you can chant a round in as little as four or five minutes.

Which Mantra Should You Chant?

Some people may think the mantra you chant does not matter. They could think that simply the practice of focus and repetition are what provide the benefit. The Vedic wisdom, as well as my experience, does not support this idea. Mantras work on many levels. One is in the meaning of the mantra, and another of the many levels is in the actual sound vibration. Different words and sound vibrations have different energies. As I explained previously, there is an exact, correlating sound and even mantra for every chakra, energy channel, and even every part of existence. Therefore, the actual words and sound vibration of mantras have power. This is why affirmations, though powerful and good, can never have the same power as actual mantras. Mantras are enhanced by intention, so it is good to have an intention and know the meaning of the mantra you are chanting. Affirmations have the intention and focus part of the mantra but not the vibrational energy, so they are naturally less powerful.

In the Vedas there are thousands of mantras prescribed. Each of them creates different results. Many of them are extremely good to chant, but some mantras are better than others. I want to give you the best mantra to chant. *Om* is a very powerful mantra, yet *om* is actually considered a seed (bhija) mantra and is generally not used alone in the east. It is often the first word of longer mantras. *Om namo naryanaya* is an example of this. I think the teaching of chanting the mantra *om* alone, without any other accompanying words or mantras, was done by some teachers to simplify the processes for people not so serious, trained, or acquainted with the Vedic wisdom. It is much easier only to recite *om* without knowing the longer, more complex mantras. I want the best for you, and though it is impossible to share everything with you in this book (that's why I make online courses and live seminars!), I don't want to hold anything back. I want you to be equipped with everything you need to advance to Passionate Enlightenment.

That is why I will share with you the most powerful mantra I know. I know thousands of mantras and have practiced them since childhood. Yet one mantra prevails and remains king. If you chant this mantra with a sincere heart, I guarantee that you will advance on the spiritual path more than you ever have before, and peace, tranquility, and clarity will inundate your life. The mantra is the Hare Krishna Mantra and it is the same mantra that a near-cult that has made the center of their "branding." But you can chant this mantra and reap immense benefit without being as extreme or strange as the Hare Krishna group. The Hare Krishna Mantra is at least 5,000 years old, and the Hare Krishna movement that we see on the side of the streets in the west, though beautiful in many ways, has only been around for about 50 years. So, my friend, rest assured that this mantra exists beyond any cult, culture group, or tradition.

I am excited to share this exquisite mantra with you:

hare krishna hare krishna krishna krishna hare hare hare rama hare rama rama rama hare hare.

This mantra is so sweet, words cannot describe. The more you practice and chant this, the more sweetness and happiness will begin to ooze from the mantra and permeate your heart. While I type this paragraph and remember this Hare Krishna Mantra, I feel an immediate warmth and softness take over my heart, my mood is uplifted, and I am relishing the seductively sweet honey-like nectar of the Divine. This sudden change of being is occurring in me simply by typing this mantra once. Image how much sweetness, happiness, and love you can feel if you were to steadily practice this mantra daily. The Hare Krishna Mantra does not only awaken a passionate loving connection with the Divine, it also has immense power to affect physical reality. A fellow monk friend of mine is a complete brain (those who know him call him a genius), and he has a very detailed way of explaining how the Hare Krishna Mantra works through the perspective of information science. He is a computer programmer and math whiz. Though seeing the world through a mathematical lens is not my forte, I remember his conclusion being that by chanting the Hare Krishna Mantra, you are affecting with the very numerical fabric of existence and enhancing your power. I see the power of the Hare Krishna Mantra work on both an energetic and a spiritual level. Energetically the Hare Krishna Mantra creates an air/prana/chi energy both in one's body and in a space or environment that is nothing like I have seen elsewhere. A person begins to glow, and a space becomes tranquil when the mantra is chanted. On a spiritual level, we all want sweetness, love, and connection, and this mantra is just that. It is the mantra that pines in a passionate, loving dance play with the Divine. "Hare" is the feminine aspect of the Divine, or Radha. This word or name, like most Sanskrit words, has a plethora of meanings. One meaning is potency, energy, and sheer power; by reciting this mantra and resonating its vibration on your tongue, you gain such power. On another level, "hare" is a name of the masculine aspect of the Divine (Krishna) and means to steal or to take way; and the mantra is a calling out to the Divine to steal your heart, mind, and body so that you can be 100 percent absorbed in Him. From another perspective, Hare is Radha, or God's girlfriend, and this Divine mantra says that love is even more powerful than God. God, the origin of all existence, becomes a beggar for love, and even God's mind and heart are stolen by the love his girlfriend, Radha or Hare.

The order of the repeated words in the Hare Krishna Mantra represents the eternal dynamic love play of Radha and Krishna, and by practicing and chanting it you can enter into a deep trance-like meditative state (samdhi) and you can witness this immensely sweet, transcendental love game of the Divine. But more than witnessing transcendence in sweet loving union, this mantra is in the vocative case, which means it is a crying or calling out in prayer. The mantra is a prayer to also enter into the pleasure pastimes of the Radha and Krishna. Of course, we cannot enter into those pastimes with a body made of the eight material elements that will die one day. We are beyond these elements and have a hidden spiritual form that can be awakened through spiritual practices. According to the 5,000-year-old Vedic wisdom, in this day and age the fastest and most practical way to realize and awaken your transcendental spiritual form is through chanting a mantra, specifically the Hare Krishna Mantra.

I have just given you some quick and brief explanations of what the first word of the Hare Krishna Mantra means. This mantra is so deep I could write an entire book on it. I know that some people will be skeptical when reading this section, and I completely understand: I have made some large claims regarding the power of this Hare Krishna Mantra. All I can say is that the proof is in the pudding. Try this mantra practice yourself with a sincere heart and you will gradually feel the effect. Another thing to think is that even if the mantra does not hold the power that I and many others experience it to have, the benefits of meditation are now understood by the larger population. Many studies have been done, and many of the world's highest performers use meditation to give them that cutting edge. So if you are a driven person and want to be super effective, you are probably doing meditation anyway, so why not do this one? It is the "premium" meditation described and prescribed in the yogic and Vedic body of knowledge, which is the source of most Eastern meditation. So even if the mantra does not have the spiritual potency and magic that I have described, you will still get all the known and unknown benefits of meditation.

Musical Kirtan Meditation

Kirtan is a musical form of mantra meditation that is done in union with others. By adding music to the mix, more aspects of the ether element are engaged and therefore there is added power. As described earlier, ether is the middle element that affects both the physical and subtle domains. Music strongly affects both the mind and the air elements. When you add mantra to music the power of the mantra is fused with the effect of music. The music acts almost like a carrier oil that delivers the effect of medicine to aching muscles. Another specialty of doing Kirtan is that it is done together with other people. All mantra chanting is not created equal. Someone who has practiced and perfected chanting a specific mantra will have more power in their mantra chanting than someone who has not. Think of it like a yoga pose: If you have never practiced yoga or practiced a particular pose, even if you do it you will not be able to get the same benefit as someone who has practiced and perfected the pose. When you do Kirtan, which is mantra meditation with others in a group, the sound of the mantras combines and creates a stronger vibrational energy. Your mantra supports and enhances their mantra, and their mantras support yours.

To do Kirtan simply sing and chant mantras in music. There are many traditional tunes and Kirtan styles that are fascinating, sweet, and fun. It's good music to listen to and, though listening to mp3s doesn't match the power experience and effect of doing a live Kirtan, they can still pacify the mind and enliven the spirit.

Mind

All spiritual practice is geared to have your mind automatically echo spiritual thoughts and feelings back to you. To have your mind echo spiritual love, you simply need to feed your mind with spiritual things, and thus your heart will follow and love will grow. Chant mantras such as the Hare Krishna Mantra, listen to spiritual music, listen to spiritual discourses, read books, attend events, and just continue doing what you are doing. The fact that you are reading this tells me that you already feed your mind with goodness. By feeding your mind with all this spiritual-ness, your heart and emotions will naturally follow and spiritual love will increase. (Kirtan downloads and links are in your bonus area, *eternaldharmabook. com/bonus*)

Intelligence

To use your intelligence as a spiritual tool, contemplate the nature of the Divine. Everyone loves when you think of them, and God is no exception. I have attempted to give you plenty of food for thought about the Divine in this book, but there is so much more. Your spiritual journey is exclusively yours. Just as you need to find your individual personal dharma and relationship with the Divine, so you will need to find what spiritual knowledge inspires you and study it until the day you die. Such search and study is loving God via the medium of intelligence.

Ego/Identity

Ego/identity—the most important element of them all. Choose to identify with a specific relationship with the Divine. The Vedic approach encourages the closest, most intimate, and informal relationships with God. You could see God as your child, your best friend, or even your dearest lover. In the spiritual lineage I come from we see the feminine Radha as our life and soul and the masculine Krishna as the dearest lover of Radha. Whenever we pray, think of, or do any type of meditation, it is always in this context. If we are having a difficult time in life, we think, "Oh beautiful Krishna, beloved of Radha, what games are you playing with me?" If we see a flower we think, "Oh I want to pick that to decorate the hair of my dearest Radha."

When you have an established identity or relationship with the Divine, all other thoughts and actions flow easily and love develops to its fullest. The most important identity that works for all of us is: "I am the eternal servant of the Divine." This identity is our truest dharma.

Desire

You are desire, simply wanting and choosing to love the Divine is everything. This world can be a difficult place, full of much darkness and suffering. Spiritual knowledge gives us hope in this often-miserable reality, but spiritual growth is something we must choose. The choice can be tough; the journey is rocky. There will be times when we are deeply inspired and motivated to love and serve, and there will be times when we just won't be. In either case, we must persevere, try, and want. From there everything will follow.

My dear friend, I would like to thank and congratulate you for taking this journey with me. I am deeply impressed that you made it this far, for the subjects covered here were not easy and light. It takes a special soul to persevere. Though we have not yet met in physicality, we have met in the mind and intelligence, and I feel connected to you. Perhaps one day by the will of the Divine our paths will cross. Until then keep growing and loving. I am rooting for you, my friend.

—Vishnu Swami, The Maverick Monk

NEXT STEPS

If you found this useful, you will probably like Vishnu Swami's other training programs. Go to *www.themaverickmonk.com* or *www.vishnu-swami.com* or call 1-800-266-5141 to attend an event, book a speech, or for free videos, articles, and online training programs.

INDEX

Abridged understanding of the
    Divine, 230-235

Action, Effective, 12, 22, 25, 54,
    128, 129, 135, 151, 201

Acupuncture, 78

Adaptation, 187

Ahankara, 175

Air, 74, 76, 81, 115-126, 128, 129,
    186, 190, 253

Alignment, 33

Alignment, dharma, 48-49

Alignment, universal, 49, 51-52

Alone, being, 17

Ambiguous jargon, 54

Attention, 108

Avatar, 241

Ayurveda, 79, 80, 101, 102, 108,
    112, 113, 117, 118 150

Being alone, 17

Being, 207-208

Beneficial Temporary Dharma,
    44, 47-48, 74, 171

Bewildered Materialist, 62-63

Bhagavan, 239-240

Blank promises, 54

Bliss, 210

Bliss, 216

Book of Five Rings, The, 78

Braman, 227-230, 232

Breath, 115

Business, dharma in, 51-52

Businesses, dharma, 99-100

Ceremonies, 174

Chakras, 80

Chi, 76, 115-126, 130-131, 186, 253

Chinese system, 74

Choices, 154

Clarity, 11, 98

Communication, 185, 246

Confidence, 91, 165

Connection with the Divine,
    55-56

Connection, 11, 37, 191, 221, 246

Consciousness, 139-140, 190

Contentment, inner, 37

Control, 66-67, 115

Core nature, 56-57

Creating, sequence in, 190

Creativity, 157

Dark Path to Power, 193-194

Dedication, 62

Desire, 94, 110-111, 147, 170-171,
    178, 182-183, 190, 205, 206,
    244, 260

Detachment, 61, 62, 144

Dharma alignment, 48-49

Dharma as religion, 36-37

Dharma businesses, 99-100

Dharma in business, 51-52

Dharma of the soul, 201-214

Dharma, 13-15, 147-148

Dharma, Beneficial Temporary,
    44, 47-48, 74, 171

Dharma, Eternal, 41-42, 44, 56,
    64, 75, 88, 171, 175, 211, 212,
    245, 251

Dharma, finding your, 41-52

Dharma, Harmful Temporary, 43

Dharma, principle of, 25-39

Dharma, rules of, 35

Dharma, Temporary, 41, 42-45

Dharma, the elements and, 180

Dimension, spiritual, 19

Discipline, 132

Discrimination, 222

Disease, 48

Distress, 59

Divide, myth of the spiritual and
    material, 59-62

Divine, a loving relationship with
    the, 237-247

Divine, connection with the,
    55-56

Divine, enlightenment and the,
    225-235

Divine, the, 71-72, 75, 78, 102,
    148-149, 155-156, 157, 158,
    159, 175, 183, 195, 205, 206,
    207, 210, 213, 215, 216, 219,
    221, 223, 249-260

Dogmatic religion, 216-218

Domain, spiritual, 201-202

Domain, subtle, 135

Dominance, 66-67

Drive, 107

Duality, 138-139, 249

Earth, 74, 75-76, 97, 98-104, 128,
    188, 190, 252-253

Economy, 91

Effective Action, 12, 22, 25, 54,
    128, 129, 135, 151, 201

Effectiveness, 12, 87

Efficacy, 48

Effort, 54

Ego, 77, 92, 147, 153, 165-178, 259

Einstein, Albert, 157

Ekadashi, 103

Elemental foundations, 83-95

Elemental Reality System, 152, 156, 159

Elemental Spectrum, 75, 161, 165

Elements, 71-82, 233, 252

Elements, dharma and the, 180

Elements, manipulating the, 189-190

Elements, physical, 97, 127, 158, 173-174

Elements, subtle, 98, 127, 137

Emotional imbalances, 150

Emotions, 140-141, 185, 246

Empowerment, personal, 12-13, 118

Energy body, 118-119

Energy medicine systems, 118

Energy, 186, 253

Enlightenment, 21, 28, 44, 61, 238-239

Enlightenment, Passionate, 25, 27-28, 32, 61, 88, 128, 129, 151, 165, 205, 250, 255

Enlightenment, stages of, 225-235

Eternal Dharma, 41-42, 44, 56, 64, 75, 88, 141, 171, 211, 212, 245, 251

Eternal existence, 207-208

Eternal knowledge, 27-28

Ether, 74, 76, 81, 127-136, 160, 185-186, 253-254

Evolution, stages of spiritual, 215-224

Existence, 28

Existence, eternal, 207-208

False ego, 74, 81, 93-94, 183-184

False pride, 57

Fast, the Ekadashi, 103

Fear, 17

Felicity, 11

Finding your dharma, 41-52

Fire, 74, 76, 97, 100, 107-114, 128, 186-187, 190, 252-253

Flow, 191-192

Focus, 132

Foundations, elemental, 83-95

Free will, 205-206

God of air, 116

God Syndrome, 64-66, 196, 202, 212, 250

Goodwill, 246

Grounding, 138

Growth, personal, 201

Growth, spiritual, 29, 53-54

Guilt, 62

Happiness, 37

Hare Krishna Mantra, 255-256, 259

Harmful Temporary Dharma, 43

Harmony, 102, 179

Hay, Louise, 150

Heart pains, 16-17

Higher purpose, 18-19

Human body, 41-42

Hurt Purest, 59-62, 63

Identity, 74, 77, 92, 93-94, 138, 147, 153, 154, 165-178, 183-184, 259

Imbalances, emotional, 150

Independence, 204

Individuality in love, 249

Individuality, 232

Information Age, 220

Information, 184

Inner contentment, 27, 132

Inner inspiration, 192

Inner intuition, 232-233

Inner truths, 154

Innovation, 187

Inspiration, 11, 246

Inspiration, inner, 192

Integration of spiritual and material, 64

Integration, 53-67

Intelligence, 74, 77, 81, 92, 94-95, 147, 151-163, 178, 184, 190, 259

Intelligence, mind vs., 152-153

Interconnectedness, 102

Intuition, inner, 232-233

Japa, 132-133, 149, 254-258

Jargon, ambiguous, 54

Joy, 210

Karma, 195

Kirtan, 133, 145, 149, 258

Knowing, 209

Knowledge systems, 128, 129

Knowledge, 27, 49, 144

Knowledge, realized vs. theoretical, 29-30

Knowledge, spiritual, 209, 260

Krishna, 244-245, 247, 253, 257

Lack of efficacy, 48

Layers of truth, 153-154

Life, 17-18, 50, 107

Light, 130

Losing your power, 87

Lost Secrets of Ayurvedic Acupuncture, The, 113

Love, 123-124, 194, 206, 210, 242-246

Love, individuality in, 249

Love, spiritual, 62, 249-260

Love, worldly, 250

Maharaja, Srila Bhaktivedanta Narayan Goswami, 15

Manifestation, stages of, 182-188

Manipulating the elements, 189-190

Mantra Meditation, 39, 132-146, 197, 214, 247, 254-258

Mantras, 22, 131-132

Material and spiritual divide, myth of the, 59-62

Material domain, 26, 60, 61, 64

Meaning, 11

Meditation, 160

Memorization, 84-86

Mind exercises, 149

Mind, the, 74, 77, 81, 92, 137-150, 154, 185, 190, 258-259

Mind, intelligence vs., 152-153

Misconceptions, 205

Moment, present, 58

Money, 90-92

Motivation, 107

Musashi, Miyamoto, 78

Music, 258

Myth of the spiritual and material divide, 59-62

Nature, core, 56-57

Neutrality, 144

Non-conscious intelligence, 158-159

Obsession, one-sided, 111

Om, 246-247

One-sided obsession, 111

Pain, 48

Pains, heart, 16-17

Paramatma, 230-235, 239-240, 252, 253

Passion, 107

Passion, sexual, 110-111

Passionate Enlightenment, 25, 27-28, 32, 61, 88, 128, 129, 151, 165, 205, 250, 255

Path, spiritual, 124-125, 155-156, 175

Paths to power, 192-196

Peace, 37, 98

Personal Dharma Code, 35

Personal empowerment, 12-13, 118

Personal growth, 201

Personal responsibility, 61-62

Physical body, 250

Physical domain, 12, 84, 86-87, 180-182, 212, 258

Physical elements, 75-76, 80-81, 97, 127, 158, 173-174

Politically correct spirituality, 218

Pope Francis I, 218

Power, 54, 107, 112-113, 115, 170

Power, losing your, 87

Power, paths to, 192-196

Power, raw, 119-123

Power, subtle, 88

Practicality, 76

Prana, 76, 115-126, 129, 130-131, 186, 253

Prayer, Paramatma and, 234

Predictability, 98

Preliminary understanding of the Divine, 227-230

Present moment, 58

Pride, false, 57

Principle of dharma, 25-39

Promises, blank, 54

Proof, 15-16

Purpose, 11, 49-52

Purpose, higher, 18-19

Radha, 244-245, 247, 252, 253, 257

Raw power, 119-123

Reality, subtle, 181

Realized vs. theoretical
knowledge, 29-30

Relationships, 92-95

Relaxation, 191-192

Religion, 55

Religion, dharma as, 36-37

Religion, dogmatic, 216-218

Responsibility, 112-113, 204-205

Responsibility, personal, 61-62

Results, 12, 54

Reverse anthropomorphization, 238

Rhythm, 76, 101

Risk, 107

Rituals, 174

Ros, Dr. Frank, 113

Routine, 101

Rules of dharma, 35

Satisfaction, 17

Self-control, 132

Self-esteem, 62, 165

Selfishness, 193

Separation, 111

Sequence in creating, 190

Service, 212

Sexual passion, 110-111

Shining Path to Power, 194,
196-197

Soul, 207

Soul, dharma of the, 201-214

Sound, 128-132, 185-186

Space, 76, 81, 127-128, 185-186

Spectrum, Elemental, 75, 161, 165

Spiritual and material divide,
myth of the, 59-62

Spiritual dimension, 19

Spiritual domain, 26, 64, 201-202

Spiritual evolution, stages of,
215-224

Spiritual growth, 29, 53-54

Spiritual knowledge, 209, 260

Spiritual love, 62, 249-260

Spiritual path, 124-125, 155-156

Spiritual path, 175

Spiritual Surrender, 14, 21, 30, 32,
53-67, 72, 213, 252

Spiritual wisdom, 18, 220-223

Spirituality, 219

Spirituality, politically
correct, 218

Stages of enlightenment, 225-235

Stages of manifestation, 182-188

Stages of spiritual evolution,
215-224

Structure, 76

Subtle body, 250

Subtle domain, 12, 84, 86-88, 95,
135, 180-182, 212, 258

Subtle elements, 76-77, 80-81, 98,
127, 137

Subtle power, 88

Subtle reality, 181

Success, 48-49, 54

Supersoul, 230, 240

Surrender, 13-15

Surrender, Spiritual, 14, 21, 30, 32, 53-67, 72, 213, 252

Sword Duel to the Death, 77-78

System, Elemental Reality, 152, 156, 159

Systems, 12-13

Systems, energy medicine, 118

Temporary Dharma, 41, 42-45

Temptation, 238

Theoretical vs. realized knowledge, 29-30

Truth, layers of, 153-154

Truths, inner, 154

Unbendable arm technique, 88-90, 117

Understanding of the Divine, 227-235

Universal alignment, 49, 51-52

Unlimited desire, 244

Unprecedented Elemental Reality System, 71-81, 83-84, 90, 129, 130, 179-197, 201, 239

Vayu, 116

Vedas, the, 15, 26-29, 30, 42, 43, 48, 65, 72-74, 78, 80, 81, 84-85, 102-104, 108, 113, 118, 123-124, 129, 130, 144-145, 148, 158, 159, 161, 174, 192, 196, 201, 203, 205, 209, 226, 231, 233-234, 239, 241, 243, 246-247, 252, 253, 255, 257-258, 259

Vibrations, 76

Vyas, 226

Water, 74, 76, 97, 100, 104-107, 128, 187-188, 190, 252-253

White light, 227-228

Wisdom, 25, 26

Wisdom, spiritual, 18, 220-223

Worldly love, 250

Yoga, 20-21, 26-27, 124-125

Yoga, Paramatma and, 233-234

You Can Heal Your Life, 150